Cristiano Ronaldo

Ronaldo

A Biography of the Portuguese Superstar

(Inspirational and Motivational Life Story of Cristiano Ronaldo)

Branson Kreiger

Published By **John Kembrey**

Branson Kreiger

Cristiano Ronaldo: A Biography of the Portuguese Superstar (Inspirational and Motivational Life Story of Cristiano Ronaldo)

ISBN   978-1-77485-908-7

Legal & Disclaimer

The information contained in this ebook is not designed to replace or take the place of any form of medicine or professional medical advice. The information in this ebook has been provided for educational & entertainment purposes only.

The information contained in this book has been compiled from sources deemed reliable, and it is accurate to the best of the Author's knowledge; however, the Author cannot guarantee its accuracy and validity and cannot be held liable for any errors or omissions. Changes are periodically made to this book. You must consult your doctor or get professional medical advice before using any of the suggested remedies, techniques, or information in this book.

Table Of Contents

Chapter 1: The Legend Of The Night Is Born

Cristiano Ronaldo dos Santitos Aveiro, born 5 February 1985, in Santo Antonio, a neighborhood of Madeira an island of a few hundred square kilometers located off the west coast of Portugal. He was the youngest children of mother Maria Dolores dos Santos along with father Jose Dinis Aveiro, was raised in the poverty of the tin roofed house and sharing his room with his three older brothers: Hugo, Elma, and Liliana Catia. He had a father who was alcohol addict and, to pay the bills, his mother was employed in two different jobs, cooking and cleaning, and the other one as cleaner.

The first name was Ronaldo is the name given to his father by his father in honor of his most beloved actor Ronald Reagan.

From the very beginning it was apparent that he was a natural for soccer and his parents knew this was the path to take him to get out of the poor neighborhoods. As a child, the player was a part of a small town club called Andorinha and there was a kit keeper and when the age of 10 He was considered to be "one to watch in the near future."

Its godfather Fernao Sousa once said to reporters "All that he ever wanted was to play soccer. He was so enthralled by the game that many times he'd skip meals and sneak from the window of his bedroom with a ball even when it was time to be working on his assignments."

After a brief stint for a brief time Primeira Liga club Nacional (based in Madeira), Ronaldo was given the chance to take part in an all-day trial for three days with Sporting CP (Sporting Clube de Portugal) Another Primeira Liga side. Sporting CP was so in love by the youngster they signed immediately for $2000. In the following year, he moved to Alcochete close to Lisbon for the youth academy of the club.

At the age of 14, He was kicked out of school for throwing a chair towards an instructor who "disrespected" his. At this point the mother of his son, Dolores, decided it was best for him to drop out of school and concentrate more on playing football.

Then, a year later, a tragedy nearly end his career when it was discovered that he had a raced heart. This is a condition that occurs when in rest the heart beats much faster than it normally does. The patient underwent surgery. the use of a laser was to treat the affected area. The patient was released from hospital after a short time. A few days later, he was back in the classroom.

Chapter 2: For The Club...

Sporting CP

At the age of 16 Ronaldo was elevated as a youth player to senior team by the coach Laszlo Boloni. Boloni said Cristiano impressed him with his ability to dribble. He became the first Sporting player that played in the Under-16s team, the under-17s the under-18s as well as the B team along with the team for Senior during the same season. In 2002 on the 7th of October 2002 Ronaldo was the first player to make his debut for Primeira Liga against Moreirense. Unexpectedly, Ronaldo scored two goals in the victory 3-0.

A specific date changed Ronaldo's life for the better. It was on August 6, 2003, when he attended the official opening of the new Sporting CP venue, Estadio Jose Alvalade. To mark the occasion, Sporting CP played English side Manchester United. Sporting defeated Manchester United 3-1 that day and were so impressed by those Manchester United players with Ronaldo that they asked the manager of their team, Alex Ferguson, to purchase Ronaldo.

In the window of transfer which came around three clubs made offers to Cristiano: Liverpool, Barcelona and Arsenal. He turned them down opting instead to trade his craft with the largest team in the English Premier League: Manchester United.

Manchester United

The fee for the transfer paid to Ronaldo at a staggering PS12.24 million ($16.2 million) was at the time the highest ever paid to an adolescent. He was also the first Premier Club's Portuguese player (followed by Nani, Bebe, and Anderson).

He had initially asked for the number. 28 shirt since that was his personal number for Sporting CP, but his request was not granted. Instead, he received the number. 7 shirt, which was worn by Manchester United legends such as Eric Cantona, George Best as well as David Beckham.

Manchester United manager, Sir Alex Ferguson, was key in the growth of Ronaldo and was a major influence when it came to his development as player. When asked about Ferguson's influence, Ronaldo stated to reporters "He's been my dad in sports which is being one of my most significant and influential elements in my professional life."

His debut in the team on August 16, 2003, against Bolton Wanderers, coming on in the 61st minute as a substitute for Nicky Butt (midfielder) and received an ovation standing up. The legendary Manchester United midfielder, George Best stated that his most thrilling debut he's ever had. The 1st November of this year Ronaldo made his debut goal at Manchester United. It was a free-kick that led to the 3-0 victory over English Premier League side, Portsmouth. The game didn't go according as planned, however with Ronaldo showing his dark side was dismissed on the final game of the year in the match against Birmingham club Aston Villa. In addition, he scored in the game.

The most coveted football trophy in England can be found in the Football Association Challenge Cup (commonly known as"the FA Cup). The cup permits every club, professional or non-professional to compete each year in a knockout style tournament. On the 22nd of May, 2004, Manchester United beat Millwall 3-1. Ronaldo's debut piece of silverware from England. Ronaldo scored the first goal in the 44th minute.

There is a saying that with every genius is an element of inequity; it's like a one might say that it's Dr. Jekyll against a Mr. Hyde. It's the same with Ronaldo. A number of incidents in the third season of his career caused anxiety. When he played in the Champions League he was booed by Benfica supporters. It was a recollection of the time he played for Benfica opponents, Sporting CP, a huge rivalry. Instead of turning away from the crowd He reacted by making an oblique salute. The result was that he was penalized $5,000 and handed one-match suspension. He also got into a fight with his another Manchester United teammate, Ruud van Nistelrooy (Dutch striker) during a session of training when van Nistelrooy was averse to his flamboyance. Van Nistelrooy was heard saying, "go crying to your daddy," a reference to Ronaldo's close relationship with Manchester United assistant manager and his fellow Portuguese, Carlos Queiroz.

An even more famous incident took place during at the time of the World Cup finals, held in Germany during which Portugal played England during the semifinals. In the 62nd minute the match, England player and Manchester United teammate, Wayne Rooney, seemed to smack Portuguese defenseman, Ricardo Carvalho. Ronaldo protested with a ferocious voice to referee Horacio Marcelo Elizondo, asking for action. After seeing the situation, Wayne Rooney pushed Ronaldo in the chestand then gave some verbal abuse as a result. Elizondo was convinced and he swiftly removed Rooney off. Ronaldo was observed a couple of minutes later wagging at his teammates sitting on the bench. Some claim that the incident was not the fault of Ronaldo at any time, given that Rooney could have been dismissed regardless however, others argue claim that Ronaldo had influenced the official. Whatever the case, it demonstrated the insanity that is Ronaldo, the Portuguese player. After the match , he publically requested a transfer to Manchester United, as he believed that Manchester United had not been supportive of his actions during the incident. The request was not granted.

The 2007 Premier League season saw Ronaldo getting booed by away supporters as well as a portion of his own supporters. It didn't bother Ronaldo, however, because the season progressed, he broke the 20-goal threshold in the very first time and took home the first Premier League title. He attributes the success of his team to coach Rene

Meulensteen, who taught him to be more flexible as well as improve his teamwork skills, play the ball, and take advantage of scoring opportunities instead of looking to score "good-looking" scores. This was an excellent advice given in the game against Premier League team, Blackburn Rovers and he was substituted and was greeted with applause. The opposition fans.

In the same season, Ronaldo achieved his first Champions League goals. They were scored in the match against Italian Serie A side, Roma. He also received the professional footballers' association's Player's (abbreviated in the form of PFA Player's Player) as well as the fans' Player, and Footballer of the Award of the Year. Additionally, he was awarded FWA's Football Writer the Award for the year. This made him the only player to be awarded the top four PFA and FWA distinctions. The result was that the club offered him a new five-year deal with Manchester United, with a weekly salary in the region of PS120,000 ($160,000) and an annual wage that was PS31 million ($42 million).

The 2007-08 season was a season in which Ronaldo was able to score 42 goals across every competition. His first goal match was against his former club Sporting CP, in the Champions League. In the second game, however his volatile nature resurfaced its ugly head. And during an Premier League game against Portsmouth the player was sent off for a head-butt to another pro Richard Hughes. The manager Alex Ferguson blasted him for being provoked, and then dismissed. He was then suspended for three games, but he refused to relent, saying that he was provoking. "I am angry because three matches are unjust. I'm willing to resist the provocation , but only for a limited time. The limit was set at Portsmouth. It was ridiculous," he was quoted as declaring. Then, he appeared to change his mind, saying the ban taught him to not allow people to provoke him.

One of Ronaldo's biggest desires was to be recognized as the greatest footballer alive. During the latter part of 2007 , his dream became a reality. Almost. He was 2nd to the Ballon d'Or (an award presented every year to the top athlete of the season) and was beaten by Brazilian Kaka. Third was his arch-rival and nemesis Lionel Messi. He also finished third to Kaka as well as Messi at the FIFA World Player of the Award of the Year.

The next year, on the 12th of January the following year, he achieved his first ever hat-trick in the history of Manchester United against Newcastle United in a 6-0 win over Newcastle United. The six goals scored were in the second half and the Portugal player scored the first score in the 48th minute. This was, however, his only hat-trick in the club.

One of the most memorable moments of his career was for Ronnie on the 19th of March in 2008 when he sat in the captain's chair of Manchester United for the first time. This was in opposition to Premier League team Bolton

Wanderers. In the 2-0 victory over Bolton, Ronaldo scored twice to bring his total at the time to 33. Ronaldo broke the record-breaking Manchester United striker George Best's record of scoring 32 goals in the season 1967/68. The 31 goals scored by him in the league contributed to Manchester United win the title and Ronaldo's second. In the same season, he was given his Golden Boot (given to a player with the highest number of goals scored in a single season) as well as the European Golden Shoe (formerly called the European Golden Boot, it is given to those who have scored the most goals across all the recognized European competitions). He was the first Winger to ever be awarded the prize.

A tense situation erupted after Manchester United filed a tampering complaint against Spanish La Liga (Spain's highest division) team, Real Madrid. United asserted they believed that the Spanish Giants were trying to sway the player. Naturally, Real Madrid denied this by claiming they had no proof. Manchester United had no proof other than speculation in the press. The article 18 in FIFA's Regulations states "that clubs that is interested in a player from another club must notify the other club in writing of its intention to negotiate with the player or players." Ronaldo, himself in the midst of serving for his country at Euro 2008, stated that the club would not discuss the issue any further while being with the Portuguese team. In the past, however it was well-known fact that he had secretly planned to sign up with the Spanish Galacticos. The then FIFA president Sepp Blatter remarked that the player should be permitted to depart Manchester United, as it was akin of "modern slavery" to keep him in the club. Although he later sided in the same way as Blatter, Ronaldo stayed with United for another year.

In 2008-09, Ronaldo had an ankle operation. He was from playing for a period of 10 weeks. After his return the following week, he got his hundredth Manchester United goal. It was scored at the hands of Stoke City. Another record was broken, since he scored against each EPL team that was playing at the time. Five days later, the player was red-carded it was his third time in the same venue, Eastlands which was Manchester City's former ground (Manchester City has since relocated to a bigger stadium which is now The Etihad Stadium). It was not a straight red. there were two yellow cards. One for a knock on Shaun Wright-Phillips. The other was for an unidentified handball. United nevertheless won the game by 1-0, despite the fact that it was a draw.

In December 2008, Ronaldo was instrumental in helping United in winning in the World Club Cup, a tournament that is a prize for champion clubs from the six continental confederations that are recognized by FIFA. The final was held in the International Stadium of Yokohama in Japan and was played against Ecuadorian team, LDU Quito, the CONMEBOL (Confederacion Sudamericana de Futebol) champions. The winner's goal came from Wayne Rooney in the 73rd minute.

After years of trying, Ronaldo finally won the sought-after Ballon d'Or in 2008, becoming one of the few United player to be awarded the prize after George Best in 1968.

A few days prior to Christmas 2009, he received the Puskas Award (an award created in 2009, to honor the memory of Hungarian footballer, Ferenc Puskas, that recognizes the most memorable goals of 2009). The award was presented to him for his thunderbolt goal against Portuguese team, Porto, in the Champions League, which he declared to be the most important achievement of his career.

In June of 2009 Manchester United fans were left shocked, but not shocked at all, when Ronaldo quit the club to Real Madrid. He left United after winning nine trophies and the three Premier League titles, and the Football League Cup.

Real Madrid

An estimated 80,000 people attended Ronaldo's appearance on the Santiago Bernabeu; Real Madrid's stadium (usually reduced to just, The Bernabeu). This was more than earlier records with 75,000 people at Diego Maradona's event when he was signed by Napoli during July 1984. He was given the number. 9 jersey by Real Madrid legend Alfredo Di Stefano. Alfredo Di Stefano originally was looking for the number. seven shirt but it was already used by Real Madrid striker Raul.

The player made debut with Real Madrid on August 29 2009, when they played Deportivo La Coruna. It was scored on the penalty area. Then he made history as the only Real Madrid player to score during his first four matches in the first four games for Real Madrid. in the Champions League that year he scored two goals, both on free kicks in the club's first game in the group in the group stage against Swiss club, Zurich.

While on duty on the international front in October, he suffered a sprain to his ankle, which caused him to be off duty over seven months. The injury was first diagnosed in September however, it was worsened in October.

After his return, a week later He was once more red-carded during his La Liga game against Almeria after receiving two yellow cards. one, a smug but now automatic yellow to take off his shirt after scoring a goal, the second, for striking the ball towards Almeria midfielder Juanma Ortiz. Later, he apologized, saying, "I'm human, and I'm human, and I've made mistakes. There are flaws in me too but I'm an athlete who doesn't like to lose or miss. I was devastated when I missed the penalty, which is why I didn't feel like celebrating the goal that came after. I'm a perfectionist, however, I am happy Karim (Benzema) has scored. I was sent off for the fact that I was reacting instinctively. I'm sorry for the incident." In the match, he scored the opening goal, scored the final goal and was able to win, but missed a penalty. Karim The Benzema was the one to score the penalty, and Madrid defeated the game 4-2. He was not able to play the next game that was crucial game in the fourth place match against Valencia.

Although he scored 33 goals across all seasons and scoring a hat-trick in the match against Mallorca the Spaniard only managed second place in the Ballon d'Or and FIFA World Player of the Year. In his first season at Los Blancos (Real Madrid's nickname"Los Blancos," which translates to The Whites in Spanish) He didn't win anything.

The next campaign, Raul surprisingly left Real Madrid to join a German team, Schalke 04. This allowed Ronaldo the chance to wear the No. seven shirt. He graciously agreed to.

On the 23rd October 2010, he scored 4 goal in a game against Racing Santander. It was the final game of a string of six games which he scored 3 times during La Liga, once in the Champions League and twice for Portugal with a total of 10 goals. It was the highest he has scored in one month. But, he wasn't considered for nomination for the Ballon d'Or that year, and it is the only time during his time in Spain that he had not been chosen.

At home, he took home his first award on the 20th of April when he was playing for Real Madrid when they beat their rivals Barcelona 1-1 during the 2010 Copa Del Rey final. It was the 109th final since the tournament was first established at the age of 1903. The match was played on the Mestalla Stadium, home to La Liga side Valencia. The match took place "El Clasico" which means a match that is traditionally played in the traditional way between Real Madrid and Barcelona. It is the 6th Copa Del Rey El Clasico final, with the previous one taking place on April 5th in 1990. It was also played in Valencia. The last time that the two teams played one another within La Liga was just four days prior. They also had to face each other during the Champions League seven days later. In the 103rd second minute of the match, Ronaldo headed the ball into the goal to secure the 18. Copa Del Rey victory.

In the tradition of teams that have won major competitions the trophy is paraded all over to the place (or town) where the football team is from, often in the open top of a double-decker bus. The winners then distribute the trophy to one the other and lift it high for the crowd to clap to. Real Madrid did exactly this. When it was Sergio Ramos's turn as defender and he fell, the cup was dropped by him. It fell just in front of his double-decker's wheel in which it was broken to pieces! Ramos later admitted that he hadn't dropped the cup, and had jumped to meet the crowd. After a month, it was replaced and was placed into the Madrid trophy cabinet alongside their other trophy and cups (and as far from Ramos as is possible surely!)

In the same year, Ronaldo equaled his personal record of scoring 42 goals across all competitions during a single season. He also broke the records of Telmo Zarra, who played predominantly in the team of Atletico Bilbao (1940-1955) and Hugo Sanchez, who initially began his career as a player at Atletico Madrid before switching colors and changing clubs towards Real Madrid. But he scored two goals against Almeria on the following weekend to surpass that record. He scored 40 goals. The match in the match against Almeria was his final opportunity to break the record. In the following year, he was awarded the Pichichi Trophy (also called Trofeo Pichichi it is awarded to the player with the most goals scored during the course of the year in La Liga by Spanish newspaper Marca and for the second time, it was the European Golden Shoe. He became the first person to win the award in two distinct leagues. The second season he played in ended playing for Los Blancos, with 53 goals across all competitions. As if that weren't enough goals, in the next season, 2011, he scored a staggering 60 goals across every competition!

Although Barcelona took home this year's Supercopa de Espana (Spanish Super Cup) 5-4 in aggregate, over Real Madrid, at Camp Nou (Barcelona's home ground) but it wasn't enough to hinder Ronnie scoring the 100th time he scored for Madrid. It helped him to regain his status among the top players in the world . the team finished second to no other than Lionel Messi in the Ballon d'Or in spite of scoring hat-tricks on Real Zaragoza, Rayo Vallecano, Malaga, Osasuna, and Sevilla. His hat-trick in Sevilla placed Madrid at the top of the league until half-way. However the next time around in Europe, Madrid was eliminated from the Champions League when his penalty kick in the shootout had to be kept by Bayern Munich's goalie Manuel Neuer. On the other hand of this coin happy, Madrid won La Liga for the first time in the span of four years, with the record-breaking score of 100 points.

His 100th goal for the club (as as opposed to 100 goals in all competitions in the past) was scored in the match against Real Sociedad. The match took place on March 24 2012, and he was able to accomplish this feat in only three matches over 92 seasons. Previous records were held by legendary, Ferenc Puskas (after whom the Puskas award is named). He scored 46 goals by the final game of the season, however at this point, it wasn't an official record, as Lionel Messi had claimed that by scoring 50 goals in the same season. However, he did beat the record for scoring against all teams of La Liga, so all was not lost.

CR7 (nicknamed because of the initials of his name and the shirt number that was given to him following Raul's departure. Raul) started the 2012-13 season by winning at the Supercopa de Espana by beating Barcelona. The teams were drawn 4-4, however Madrid was able to win by scoring away goals. It was the third time he had won a trophy in Spain. In the match, he scored in both legs and scored that he had scored 150 goals for his club. However he was unable to celebrate the achievement, blaming an "professional problem" at the club he wasn't happy about. The incident didn't dampen his enthusiasm when the striker scored his first hat-trick during the Champions League in a 4-1 victory over Dutch club Ajax. Additionally, he became only player in history to have scored a string of six consecutive Clasicos when he scored two goals (two goal) to make it at 2-2. However his team was third to the Ballon d'Or to...Lionel Messi.

Contrary to unlike the English Premier League, teams in Spain are not able to play football in winter. Following this break in 2012-13, Ronaldo took over the captaincy of Madrid at first. The match took place with Real Sociedad in a 4-3 victory. On the 30th of January 2013 Ronaldo became the first non-Spaniard to be the captain of Madrid at El Clasico.

This was his 500th game in the team. A few days earlier, in a match against Getafe and in which the striker scored a hat-trick the player scored 300 goals for every club which he was a part of. He scored his 200th goals for Madrid was scored on May 8 during an 6-2 win against minnows Malaga. He scored the goals in just 197 games.

He also played a role in helping Madrid reach their Copa Del Rey final by defeating Barcelona during El Clasico. He scored two goals as the only player in six games in a row against Barcelona. It was twice more than any other player.

Additionally, in the Copa Del Rey final against Atletico Madrid He scored the first goal in the game but only for Madrid to lose the game by a score of 2-1. This was for the very first time since 14 seasons that Atletico had defeated their rivals. He was sent off seven times in the 114th minutes of the match after he clashed with Atletico Gabi. Gabi (again). In the year, Madrid did not defend their league title and lost to rivals Barcelona.

In the first knockout phase in the Champions League in 2012-13 Madrid was up against Ronaldo's former Manchester United club. Manchester United. Ronaldo scored twice: once to draw level, and another time to secure the win. He later stated that he was disappointed to have lost his old club, which he loved dearly from the tournament. Madrid however were knocked out in the semi-finals with Germans, Borussia Dortmund. Ronaldo was in the position of Champions League top-scorer for the second time in a row, scoring 12 goals. He scored 55 goals across every competition.

Rumors and rumors of his going away were prevalent, but soon put to rest when he signed a fresh three-year contract that will run the player to the year 2018. The amount he earned was increased by EUR17 million ($20 million) net, which made him the highest-paid footballer around the globe (David Beckham, who was also the highest-paid player at the time he signed for MLS club LA Galaxy that year).

The time came when English club Tottenham Hotspur sold Welsh international Gareth Bale to Real Madrid for a world record EUR100 million ($117 million, making Bale the world's highest-priced player) in addition to French team Lyon traded Karim Benzema to Lyon for

EUR8 million ($8.6 million) The three players made an unstoppable trio on the opening day. They were dubbed by the press BBC because of their initials: Bale, Benzema, Cristiano. Ronaldo declared that he was in top form for his lifetime at that point. It's not hard to believe thissince Ronaldo scored 32 goals over 22 matches , both for his national and club. He finished the season scoring 69 goals over the 59 games. A personal record. He was awarded the Ballon d'Or that year establishing himself as the top soccer player of all time. It's important to note that the press did vote for the Bayern Munich's Franck Ribery to win the award. Ribery also played a role in helping Madrid achieve La Decima, their tenth European Cup.

The Champions League he recorded his 100th match in the tournament and surpasses Lionel Messi's record for fourteen Champions League goals when he scored against Borussia Dortmund.

Other records were broke when he was awarded a penalty in the match against La Liga side Atletico Madrid to become the first player to score in two European Cup finals for two teams from two different leagues (Real Madrid and Manchester United). He was extremely calm in the match however, because there was a problem known as Patellar Tendinitis, or jumper's knee. This condition is caused by people who regularly jump. It is believed to be linked with ankle injuries and painful ankle movements, something that Ronaldo was prone to previously (it could also be due to hamstring injuries). Ronaldo did not follow medical advice and stated, "In your life, you cannot succeed without sacrifices, and you have to be willing to take risks."

The following year in the following season, he was the top scorer during the Champions League with 17 goals and was awarded UEFA's Best player for the Year in Europe award. The Copa Del Rey he helped Madrid get to the final, when scoring twice in the final against Atletico Madrid. The first goal signified that he scored in every minute of the 90-minute match which he was a part of. However, recurring issues caused by his knee prevented him from participating during the Copa Del Rey final where Real Madrid beat Barcelona 2-1. Madrid finished the season third this year, however Ronaldo was a major contributor to the cause, scoring 31 goals over the course of 30 games. The feat was recognized with a second prize within the Pichichi and European Golden Shoe category. He was required to share his European Golden Shoe award with Barcelona's Luis Suarez, however. At this point, he had recorded 400 goals over 653 games for his country and clubs. On the 6th January 2014, the striker scored two goals in a game against Celta Vigo. The goals were dedicated to Portuguese legendary footballer Eusebio who died the previous day. A deft back-heeled strike at Valencia the 4th of May won the player the top strike of the year from Liga de Futbol Profesional (Spain's football body).

They also awarded him the title of the best soccer player of La Liga.

The following season Ronaldo set a new personal record in scoring 61 goals across all competitions, beginning with two goals in the win against Sevilla during the UEFA Super Cup. In the month of December, Ronaldo scored his 23rd hat-trick in a game against Celta Vigo making him the fastest player to score 200 points in Spanish division. He did this feat in only 178 games. He also took home his third Ballon d'Or, joining the likes of Michel Platini, Johann Cruyff as well as Marco van Basten as a three-time winner of the prize.

2015-16 couldn't have been any worse than it was for Real Madrid. Their winning streak of 22 matches ended with a loss at Valencia (2-1) They failed to win any trophy throughout the entire season, losing in the semis in the Champions League and to top the season off, they finished last to last in La Liga, to Barcelona of all teams. But, Ronaldo furthered his record of scoring consecutive goals in away games , which now stands at 12, which included both goals in their loss in the final against Italian titans Juventus. He scored 10 goals during the Champions League that year, being the top scorer with Neymar and Messi for the third consecutive season in which he did so.

The first time he scored five goals was on April 5 , against Granada. The streak included an eight-minute hat trick. Granada was beaten 9-1. He scored his 300th goals to Real Madrid came just three days later, against Rayo Vallecano. He set the record for the most hat-tricks scored by Real Madrid when he scored against Sevilla, Espanyol, and Getafe. This was his 31st hat trick for the club, and he beat Angelo Di Stefano's record of 28 triples. The season was concluded by scoring 48 times. Alongside being awarded the Pichichi award for the second time in succession He also took home the European Golden Shoe for a record-breaking fourth time.

On the 12th of September in 2015, he was the all-time top goalscorer for Real Madrid with five goals against Espanyol and bringing his total to 230 goals over more than 203 games. He surpassed the previous record holder, Raul. He also set a record for the most goals scored at the Champions League when he scored three goals during the game against Ukrainian side Shakhtar Donetsk. Donetsk scored 80 goals during the competition and beat the previous record-holder, Messi, on 77. On September 30, he scored two goals against Swedish team, Malmo, to reach 500 goals, both for team and country.

The following month, on October 17 , he overtook Raul in scoring the second goal of the 3-0 victory over Levante on the Bernabeu. The score brought his total to 324 goals across all games for Madrid.

In Europe the player has scored 16 times in the Champions League making him the highest scorer for the fourth time in a row. season. The fitness issues he was suffering from again affected him, and he did poorly when he played in the Champions League final against Atletico Madrid. He , however, score a penalty in the final match, and secured La Undecima, the 11th victory for Madrid.

For the sixth consecutive season He recorded more than 50 points in every format of competition.

Chapter 3: And Country

Ronaldo started the international stage in the year 2001 when he was 16 years old. He has played in all clubs of his national team, which includes the under-17s, under-15s and under-15s as well as the under-23s, under-21s, and under-20s and, of course, the senior squad. As a young man He was a captain of 34 national teams as well as scored 31 goals. He also participated in his first 2004 Olympics held in Athens, Greece.

He was drafted into the senior team when he was only 18 years old. He was playing his first international match against Kazakhstan. It was on the 20th of August the 20th of August, 2003. His first international goal was against Greece during the group stages of the European qualifying in preparation for Euro 2004. Greece won the final of the tournament. In the European qualifying section of the 2006 World Cup, held in Germany In the final, he was the second highest scorer, scoring seven goals. He also had his very first World Cup goal when Portugal played Iran. The goal came from the spot.

On the 6th of February, 2007, one day following his birthday of 22 years old the captain was elected by Portugal in a friendly match against Brazil. It was a request made by Carlos Silva, the president of the Portuguese Football Federation, who was tragically killed just two days earlier. The request was made in his final hours prior to his death. To show honor, Ronaldo did not celebrate his birthday in the year he died. In the game, Ronaldo was continually being beaten in the game by Brazilians and was forced been substituted at 62 minutes in order to avoid injury and also for his own safety.

Following the departure of Portuguese manager, Luiz Felipe Scolari (after losing to Germany 3-1, at the Euro 2008 final), Carlos Queiroz replaced him. Queiroz was his assistant in the past at Manchester United, remember, and Ronaldo was an elder persona. Ronaldo was appointed captain permanent in July of 2008, but during the European qualifying matches for the World Cup 2010 he failed to score even a single qualifying goal.

In the World Cup, he was awarded Man of the Match for all three games in the group stage against Cote d'Ivoire (the Ivory Coast), North Korea, and Brazil. His only goal in the tournament came to beat North Korea in a 7-0 beating. It was his first goal in the international arena for over 16 months. Portugal's quest ended with a 1-0 defeat by their neighbors Spain in the final 16.

His record for qualification improved the subsequent campaign, when the player scored 8 goals in the quest to reach World Cup 2014 in Brazil and on the 17th of October 2012, he scored his 100th cap with an 1-1 draw against Northern Ireland. Northern Ireland may well have been a good sign for him, as he made his debut hat-trick of his country against them, during the span of 15 minutes, on the 6th of September, 2013. It was the return qualifier match in Portugal that Portugal beat the Irish 4-2.

Portugal did not qualify automatically to participate in the World Cup 2014 and instead needed be playing Sweden in an impromptu play-off. This was a stressful moment for the Portuguese because a loss would result in them being eliminated during the qualification phase. An embarrassing result, no doubt. But it was Ronaldo to save the day as the striker scored all four goals in the rout to the Swedes. The hat-trick he scored in the second game meant that Ronaldo had increased his total international score to 47, which is equal to the legendary Portuguese striker Pauleta's record. They had qualified. However, only a little. He also broke Pauleta's record by scoring two goals in a friendly game against Cameroon.

The same old problems resurfaced and Patellar Tendinitis came back. To top it off there was an injury to his thigh. He played on, however he said, "If we had two or three Cristiano Ronaldos on the team I'd feel more at ease. But we don't." He was very humble!

He was on the field for all time of 90 minutes during the match against Germany however he did not stop his team from losing 4-1. After a 2-2 score in the game against United States, he popped in to score the winner against Ghana with a score of with a score of 2-1. It was fifty international goals for Portugal and was his first Portuguese who scored and be a star during the three World Cups. However, Portugal was eliminated from the tournament following the group stage, based on goal different.

Five goals and a goal in the qualification stage against Armenia was the result of him scoring 23 goals during the European Championship and, including qualifying matches, he become the tournament's top goalscorer. He also surpassed Luis Figo as his country's most-capped player , with 128 caps.

Two assists and two goals in the draw 3-3 against Hungary The Portuguese made history as the very first goal scorer in all four tournaments of the European Championship, having made record-breaking 17 appearances at the tournament. Portugal came in third place, after Iceland and Hungary usually resulting in the elimination from the tournament , but due to the newly "widened" structure (meaning that more teams were able to be eligible to participate and qualify, and instead of the two teams that qualified the top three teams went through) that meant that they been able to qualify for the final stage.

In the knockout stage of the game against Croatia, Ronaldo created very little. His sole shot was direct at Croatian goalkeeper Danijel Subasic, but this was not enough. The ball bounced off the gloves of Subasic and towards substitute Ricardo Quaresma, who slotted into the net in the 117th minute. After they defeated Poland by penalty (5-3), Ronaldo became the first player to take part for the three European Championship semifinals.

The semifinal match that is to follow against Wales will be an interesting match...

Record-signing Portuguese winger Cristiano Ronaldo, played alongside record-signing Welsh winger Gareth Bale. Both had a lot the common. Both were Wingers. Both were record-signings at that time. They had both almost entirely helped get them to semi-finals. They both were part of Real Madrid.

The stage was set. The adrenaline was racing in addition, the Stade de Lyon, where the match was being played was buzzing with anticipation. It marked the first time ever in the history of Wales that Wales had made it to the semifinals in a major football tournament. In fairness, Wales had the passion and had the best first half however, it was Portugal that took the lead after the break in the 2nd. With Ronaldo scoring the opener at the end of 50 minutes an attempt to score from an angle and Nani taking the ball toe-to-foot following a misplaced shot from Ronaldo in the 53rd minute Portugal defeated Wales with a 2-0 win. The goal scored by Ronnie in this match has made him the all-time leading scorer in the tournament alongside Frenchman, Michel Platini. Both netted nine times.

There was also a wonderful moment following the whistle blew after the whistle had been blown, when Ronaldo was able to go towards the Real Madrid teammate, Bale who was able to hold his hand and talk to him for a few minutes in what was believed to be an expression of gratitude and appreciation for the manner in which Wales had performed throughout the tournament.

Unfortunately, the worst happened to Ronaldo during the final match against France. At the end of 25 minutes Ronaldo was repeatedly slapped by French player Dmitri Payet. The French player was taken off the field for treatment. After several treatments, he tried to continue playing but ultimately was forced off and substituted with Ricardo Quaresma. However, the score was 0-0 when the final whistle, and overtime was needed been scheduled for.

Despite being severely bandaged, Ronaldo was seen throughout the remainder of the match running around, calling out his teammates and encouraging players to score. Ederzito Antonio Macedo Lopes or Eder as he's more famously known, may have been able to hear his captain. In the 109th minute the game , he put the ball into the net to give Portugal ahead 1-0 and win victory over the French at home. As captain of the team Ronaldo carried the trophy in celebration of Portugal's first major tournament win. Ronaldo was named his Silver Boot for being the second-highest goal scorer with three goals, as well as providing three assists, in addition, Portugal was named the Team of the Tournament. It marked the third consecutive time Ronaldo was part of a team named.

Chapter 4: Do I Want To Compare Thee...

Cristiano Ronaldo, it it has been stated previously was widely regarded as one of the best footballers that have ever played and the preceding chapter highlighted this fact very clearly. But this claim is in dispute among many. Others think he might not be the greatest athlete to ever play, but rather , the second greatest. Why? A different player has been arguing his position with a lot of conviction as well. His name: Lionel Messi.

Personally the two players are not more different. Ronaldo is Portuguese to begin with and Messi is Argentinian. Ronaldo plays for La Liga side, Real Madrid. Messi is a player for their rivals, Barcelona. Ronaldo is 6'1 tall. Messi stands 5'7. Ronaldo is bold often volatile and arrogant, whereas Messi is humble, shy and forgiving. Their football records are awe-inspiring. Here's a small portion of their stats in order to compare them side-by-side:

Both made it to the two Champions League finals.

The two teams regularly exceed the 50 goals-per-season threshold.

Both forwards.

Messi has been awarded the record-breaking four Ballon d'Or awards, consecutively. Ronaldo has won threeawards in succession. In the time that Messi took the title, Ronaldo was runner-up; in 2012 and 2011, he was runner-up. In 2011, and 2012, when Ronaldo was victorious, Messi was runner-up.

Ronaldo has played in 673 club appearancesand scored 487 times. Messi has had 531 appearances, scoring 487 times. Messi has made 531 appearances and scored 453 goals.

Ronaldo has been awarded 12 club awards and Messi 21.

For the stakes for all honors Ronaldo's numbers add up to 101, while Messi's is 62.

Ronaldo has played for his country at 119 times and scored 52 goals. Messi? 113 appearancesand scoring 55.

Their estimated worth: Ronaldo $221 million, Messi $210 million.

This list could go into the next. It's hard to distinguish the two. If hairs were divided, it could be said it is the case that Messi has a higher goal-to-game ratio, however that's not the most you can do. It all comes down to their personalities when it comes to the two. Are you a fan of extroverted players who play with unpredictability an enthralling passion so strong that they're more likely to be dismissed instead of calm gentlemen who do the job efficiently and with confidence, without pretenses or gimmicks? It's a difficult choice and it all depends on your personal the player you prefer.

In the past, Ronaldo was blamed for diving. The former Real Madrid manager Jose Mourinho told reporters "Cristiano is a player that is not part of the culture of the pool. there is no model of life, he is a British-trained athlete, Ferguson trained. In certain instances the simulators receive more protection, but honest players are usually the losers. I'm not being a hypocrite when I claim it is true that "they (defenders) are hitting Cristiano with a lot of force and the yellow cards never show up or are slow in getting there." However the manager of Ronaldo of Manchester United, Sir Alex Ferguson was not a fan of him at the beginning of his career, for being self-centered and extravagant.

Messi has however said there was no competition between Messi and Ronaldo in a statement that reads, "It is only the media, the press who want us to be at odds but I've never had a fight with Cristiano." In 2012, Ronaldo stated about his rival "I believe we can push each other in competition. This is why the level of competition is extremely high."

It appears that there isn't any rift. Ronaldo has said, when confronted about the relationship he has with Messi: "We don't have an unofficial relationship outside of the world of football, as we don't have any relationships with the majority of the other footballers," he remarked, but he did say that in the years to come the two of them will take a look at as a "rivalry" and be jolly about it. "We must look at this competition with optimism because it's a great way to look at it," he said.

The Jonathan Ross Show (a UK chat show) presenter in 2015, Ross inquired of Ronaldo regarding his son Cristiano Ronaldo Jr. And, what Ronaldo would do if he returned home with an Messi tattooed on his arm. Ronaldo smiled and said, "No problem. If he says this, he's clever because he is aware of his best players," to which the British fans cheered him on with a massive applause.

There are always reports of gossip regarding the greatest athletes. One only has to look at Ali-Frazier and Borg-McEnroe for some great examples. A hilarious one was going around in the beginning of 2000s. Messi was in one of his numerous interview when he got confronted by one journalists about his thoughts on the remarks made by Ronaldo who claimed that he was instructed from God to join the football team. Messi laughed at this and considered it for a moment before shaking his head . He then responded, "I don't remember telling him that." The journalists were in complete hysterics. If it's true or not it's nonetheless a hilarious story that illustrates the rivalry, true or not, between each of the players.

In a debate held at the Oxford Union in the UK in October of 2013, FIFA President Sepp Blatter was asked whether the player he prefers was Ronaldo rather than Messi. Blatter acknowledged the dedication of Messi and praised the work ethic of Argentine before making a snide comment about

Ronaldo in a statement that claimed "one of them is paying more costs for hairdressers that one." Real Madrid demanded an apology and was granted one.

Never one to shy away from controversy, during the match against La Liga team Sevilla, Ronaldo gave a mock-salute following the scoring of an injury penalty following Blatter had declared him"a "commander" in the field (possibly saying that Ronaldo was a tyrant and demanding).

Chapter 5: Personal Speaking

The father of Ronaldo, Jose, was a well-known alcohol user. He died in 2005. died due to an alcohol-related liver disease. He was only 52 years old. When he passed away, Ronaldo was quoted as declaring "I'm in no way complaining. It's just the way it is. Of of course, as I mention in my film (released at the end of November, 2015) I'd like to have a more loving father in this manner (but) it's how it goes. I'm obliged to honor his decisions as well as the choices I've made in my life and I'm content since they (taught) me a lot including him, my mom and my brothers . I'm happy You know, I have him on my mind every day, but life is that way. We must respect the decisions he made, and when I talk to him about his life, I am extremely proud, since I am so proud of him because he (taught) me a lot of things and it's amazing. I'm not disappointed I'm just so content."

One month after his father's passed away in October, a rumor was made public, alleging that the man had raped a woman in an iconic London Hotel after Manchester United had played Fulham the previous day. The woman claimed to have been sexually assaulted within the Penthouse Suite at the hotel that was in question. After an interview, Ronaldo was released on bail until further investigation. Ronaldo denied the allegations and after an investigation took place, those charges were dismissed in the hands of Scotland Yard in November 2005. Ronaldo issued a statement stating, "I have always strongly denied any wrongdoing. I am happy that this case has been resolved to allow me to concentrate on my football career at Manchester United."

On the 17th of June in 2010, Ronaldo became a father for the very first time. The son was given the name Cristiano Ronaldo Sr. and was nicknamed "Cristianinho" by his family members. Cristiano Jr. was born in the United States and for a his mother, who was not known. While her name wasn't known, it is believed that she worked as an employee of a restaurant and was awarded $15.1 million for signing a confidentiality contract and grant Ronaldo the right to guard him for life. Ronaldo has also told his son he'll disclose his mother's identity once the time comes for him to turn 18. There were rumors of a son who was who was also from the US but they were promptly dispelled through his maternal grandmother, Dolores Aveiro.

His other victories include: English models Alice Goodwin and Gemma Atkinson, Big Brother UK star Imogen Thomas, as well as socialite Paris Hilton. Since 2010, he's been in a relationship with Russian fashion model Irina Shayk. She was a model was introduced to him by way of the Armani Exchange campaigns. They both were in Vogue's cover Spanish issue in 2014, but ended up breaking from each other in January of 2015.

Ronaldo claims that he does not drink. In July 2008, he filed a lawsuit against a British tabloid, The Daily Mirror, for significant damages after they published an article entitled "Ron the Lash." (In The UK when you go out with the intent of drinking , you're considered to be "On the lashing"). The newspaper reported that Ronaldo went to the club where he was drunk on PS10,000 bottles of vodka and champagne. He had already drunk four glasses red wine while dining earlier in the evening. The incident occurred while recovering after an ankle injury, and was on crutches. The paper claimed that he had taken a trip to dance on the floor, where the dancers had taken off his crutches and danced with his feet on the floor. The newspaper paid him an undisclosed sum since he claimed that he had actually been in the club but was not a drinker. The newspaper offered to apologize. Ronaldo said he believed he'd been acquitted and now viewed the matter as resolved.

Ronaldo has said previously that he doesn't like having people around him since he's an individual, however there are some close friends. He claims it is his preference to train on his own in addition, because it's in keeping the way he lives his living. "In the game I do not have a lot of friends." the player was quoted as saying "People I believe in? Very few. The majority of the time, I'm by myself. I think of myself as an isolated person."

He, as well as all of his family members, are Roman Catholics. He is not averse to tattoos since it will hinder him from donating blood, which he gives every year several times.

In August of 2015 , he determined that he needed a new place to call home, so when he was staying in New York he bought an $18.5 million apartment located in Trump Tower.

American publication, Forbes is the only business magazine in America that has listed Ronaldo as the top player on their list of most highly paid footballers. In 2013-14, his total earnings, including salary as well as bonuses and off-field earnings , were approximately $73 million. The following year , his earnings was increased to $79 million, putting him ahead of only middleweight boxer, Floyd Mayweather Jr. as the most highly-paid athlete in the world.

SportsPro has rated him as the 5th most accessible athlete in 2012 with Barcelona's Neymar leading the list. Also, in 2014, he was included as a member of Time 100, Time magazine's annual list of the top 100 most influential individuals in the world. In June 2016, he was voted the most famous person in the world by ESPN.

Being so popular and commercially viable, sponsors began clamoring for his name and his signature, including US sports giant Nike. Ronaldo has been wearing Nike Mercurials for the entirety of his playing career and has switched between Vapor as well as Supply depending on which one is the most coveted model of the day. Nike has, since the year 2010 made boots specifically designed for Ronaldo and the first was The Superfly II Safari CR7 (a little slangy name, but they're selling!).

He's received sponsorships from Coca-Cola, Emporio Armani, Castrol, Banco Espirito Santo, Motorola, Jacob & Co, KFC, Tag Heuer, Fly Emirates, Samsung, Herbalife, and Pokerstars.

He's also been the main character in video games, including Pro Evolution Football 2008, Pro Evolution Football 2012 and Pro Evolution Football 2013. The actor also appears on EA Sports' FIFA video game series and its spinoff brand FIFA Street featuring throughout every match ever since FIFA Football 2004 and also on the front cover of FIFA Street 2. The series prior to that features Ronaldo's "Thigh Flex" (FIFA 13), "The Bear" (FIFA 14), "Calm Down" (FIFA 14) and "Right Here. Today" (FIFA 15) celebrations.

In terms of social media is in the realm of social media, he's got over 49 million followers on Twitter and more than 87 million Instagram followers and 119 million followers on Facebook. With a total of 25 million fans.

He has had a number of works written by him including his autobiography titled Moments which was published in 2007 and also appeared in a variety of documentaries, including Cristiano Ronaldo A World on His Feet and which was narrated by the actor Benedict Cumberbatch. Then there was Ronaldo, a documentary that focused on his life as well as his career. The movie premiered in November 2015.

Chapter 6: Good Causes

The destruction that was caused in 2004 by an Indian Ocean earthquake and tsunami caused in 2004 shocked the world. A boy aged eight known as Martunis sporting the No. 7 Portuguese football shirt , was left orphaned amid the chaos that followed. He was left for 19 days following the fact that his parents along with two other brothers died in the aftermath. He was then forced to drink puddles of water and eat noodles that he was able to find lying in the sand. Journalists finally located him, but he was so dehydrated that he was given the drip of saline. One of the members of the Save the Children team who was able to transport him to hospital said that had he been discovered within a day, the boy probably wouldn't be alive today.

When he saw the destruction on television, Ronaldo went to Martunis his village in Banda Aceh, in Indonesia and met the young boy.

Martunis explained to Ronaldo the story of how he was playing soccer during the 9.3 magnitude earthquake. Ronaldo was later heard to tell reporters "I think that a lot of adults will not be able with what he's been through. We must be respectful of his courage. It actions were a sign of courage and maturity. He's a special child." He immediately began to raise funds to rebuild and rehabilitate the region. Martunis' home was restored with funds raised by the Portuguese FA as well as Ronaldo's efforts to raise money. Martunis was eventually reunited with his father.

11 years ago, after Tsunami hit, Sporting Lisbon, of Portugal which had trained Ronaldo during his early days (as as Luis Figo), signed Martunis to their academy of football. Martunis who is now 17 was pursuing his dream of being a footballer despite his difficulties. They had been realized.

Ronnie was a plaintiff in a lawsuit against Another British publication, The Sun, in 2008.

The Sun won the case and gave the unspecified amount to a charity in his home town of Madeira. In the following year, he received the devastating news the fact that his wife, Dolores, had been diagnosed with breast cancer. Fortunately, the tumor was successfully removed and Dolores recovered fully. To show his gratitude to the hospital that saved his mother's lives, Ronaldo gave them $234,000 in order to establish a cancer centre in the island of Madeira in which they had their headquarters.

As of 2012 Cristiano traded in the 2011 Golden Boot. He took home EUR1.5 million ($1.7 million) and donated the proceeds to Gaza for them to finance education for children. One month later, in December, he enrolled in his participation in the "11 to Health" program, which aimed to raise awareness among children, and taught children how to stay away from conditions such as addiction to drugs HIV, Malaria, and obesity.

He was also a part of the "11 to Ebola" campaign along with several other well-known footballers, including Neymar (Barcelona), Gareth Bale (Real Madrid), Xavi (Barcelona) as well as Didier Drogba (at the time of the English club, Chelsea). The campaign's slogan was "Together we can Beat Ebola." The campaign was carried out in collaboration together with Confederation of African Football and health experts. The players displaying eleven posters to increase awareness of the illness and methods to beat it.

In the following year, he was the new Save the Child's International Artist Ambassador. He stated that he was hoping to tackle the issue of children's obesity and hunger. He is also an spokesperson of Mangrove Care Forum. Mangrove Care Forum in Indonesia which is a non-profit organization that focuses on making people aware of mangrove conservation. He was honored in 2015 when he won the title of the most charitable athlete in the world.

Ronaldo established the museum in 2013 when he opened a museum. It was created to celebrate his life and his football achievements and houses all his trophies, cups and memorabilia. It is located in his home town that is located in Funchal, Madeira and is named Museu CR7.

In January of 2014 , the president of Portugal, Anibal Cavaco Silva was elevated by Cristiano to the rank of Grand Officer in the rank from Prince Henry, "to distinguish an athlete of international renown who has become a symbol for Portugal internationally, helping to the global image of the country , and providing a model of determination to the future generations."

In addition to this generousness, he gave the entire 600,00 euros ($660,000) Champions League bonus to several charities, following Real Madrid won the 2015-16 Champions League final beating Atletico Madrid 5-3 in penalties following an 1-1 draw.

Chapter 7: What's Is Next?

Ronaldo is currently 31. He has a few years to play as a soccer player, with the majority of players retiring in their thirties. The question may have been on his mind. What happens next after the game?

The man is famous for his style and is thought of by many as an icon of fashion. The year 2006 was the time he launched his first boutique of fashion on Madeira Island. Madeira as"CR7" (his name and his shirt's number). The popularity of the shop that an additional store was established within two years in Lisbon. His products include diamond-studded belts and jeans with pockets made of leather, and the patented buckled loafers. The brand has expanded called CR7 by launching a line of shoes and shirts. The brand also offers a selection of socks and underwear which he co-designed along with New York fashion designer, Richard Chai, and he recently launched a scent together and Eden Perfumes called Legacy (which smells amazing, by the way!).

Of course this isn't enough to satisfy Cristiano. He has since launched the chain of luxury hotels with the name CR7. The first three hotels will be at Funchal, Lisbon, and Madrid The fourth is scheduled, which is not surprising, with the intention of opening in New York. The chain will be operating in collaboration together with the Portuguese Pestana Hotel Group.

In the context of this, Ronaldo stated, "My job is to play football, however, life will not always be this way. I'm required to devote my time and energy to this new endeavor and I'm blessed with the most experienced team of all time in my corner, to complete it. I'm young and yet I feel extremely satisfied, and this endeavor is very exciting for me. I'm considering my future as well as my son and my family."

A hotel of the first kind is expected to open in his home town of Madeira during the summer of 2016. The hotel will then follow by Lisbon in the later part of the year. Madrid is the next destination. Madrid site is scheduled to be open by the end of the year 2017.

When asked about his contribution in the project Ronaldo jokedthat "I will be looking after all the bed!" before adding, "I am going to have the chance to be there as the projects are completed, but obviously, I don't have much time to devote in the moment however, this is all about quality. I am all focused on high-quality. I'm sure that this investment will be one of the best deals I can profit from in the near future. We had only considered one hotel in the beginning, so starting with four locations is an enormous start. It's like playing soccer for the first time, and then suddenly scoring many goals. It was a natural thing and gave me confidence in this venture, and that's the reason when you ask me about the future, I'm not sure."

Many were stunned by the fact that he did not have plans of opening an hotel in

Manchester in the city of which he has the most fond memories. However, there's an opportunity to open a hotel at New York in 2017, which has led to speculation about a possible transfer to the MLS which could be with New York City FC or the New York City FC or New York Red Bulls. The strength was added to the story when he bought a house located in New York.

6.8. Captain CRISTIANO RONALDO SUCCESSFULLY FINISHES HIS 2007/08 SEASON by leading Portugal to the quarterfinals of the 2008. UEFA EUROPEAN CHAMPIONSHIP AND WINS A EUROPEAN CHAMPIONSHIP MAN of the Match Award.

While Cristiano's season as a club player had been over His 2007/08 season wasn't completed when he joined the Portugal team to participate in their EURO 2008 tournament in Switzerland. In the final warm-up game before the tournament, Cristiano was designated the temporary Captain for Portugal's National Team. Portugal National

Team and given the number 7 shirt, which was put on rest due to the resignation of legendary Team Captain Luis Figo. In May of 2008 Cristiano began the friendly match in the match against Georgia in the Estadio Municipal do Fontelo, and was able to lead Portugal win 2-0. opening half victory as he was not playing for Quaresma after the conclusion of the first period and the match concluded with the same score. Portugal started the EURO 2008 campaign by playing against Turkey in their first game of Group A on the 7th of June in 2008 at the Stade de Geneve, as Captain Cristiano took on the entire match and helped lead the team in a 2-0 victory. In June 11th, 2008 in their second group A fixture against Czech Republic on the Stade de Geneve, Captain Cristiano took part in the entire match and was the one to provide the assist for their initial strike in the eight minute. This allowed Portugal the advantage in the opening half, however, the Czechs scored a second goal after the first period, which ended at 1-1. In the second period, Captain Cristiano showed leadership when he scored the second goal of their match in the 63rd minute , to bring them back to the top of the table before helping with their 3rd goal, in the 90th minute, ensuring Portugal's 3-1 win and the top spot in Group A, with six points. In recognition of his outstanding performance during the game, Cristiano was awarded the Man of the Match Award. Despite Cristiano's outstanding display in their final Group A match, he was not selected by coach National Team Head Coach, Scolari who was in charge of their final Group A match against hosts, Switzerland, which comprehensively defeated the non-Cristiano-playing Portugal with a score of 2-0. The defeat was the end of Portugal that only advanced into the quarterfinals due to their previous two wins, which made them the second team in their group and forced them to play the eventual finalist, Germany, in the next round.

When Portugal played their Quarterfinal match against Germany on the 19th of June 2008, when their opponents were ahead 2-0 in the opening part of the match, as a big Game Player Captain Cristiano was credited with three assists and his fourth direct goal participation in the tournament for Portugal's opening shot in the fourth minute. He did this to give his team a boost and allowed his team to draw in the 2nd half 1-1 even though they lost the game by a score of 3-2 and were eliminated from EURO 2008. Portugal's early withdrawal from the competition was due in large part to the situation that Portugal's best-known goal scorer and assist maker, Cristiano, was not involved in the match against Switzerland in an easy game that required only to draw to be first in their group. This was the reason for the removal of Luiz Felipe Scolari shortly after the end of the tournament. The replacement was the Portuguese, Carlos Queiroz, who was previously the assistant manager for Cristiano's Manchester United. In the first month of the July 2008 The new head coach named Cristiano Ronaldo the Captain of the Permanent Team of the Portugal National Team. Cristiano's one goal and three assists totalling 4 direct goal involvements over 3 games of 270 minutes at EURO 2008. This meant that he three goals scored and given five assists, resulting in an overall 8 direct goal involvements in 700 minutes over nine EURO career appearances in two editions. That's an average of one goal per 233.33 minutes, 1 assists every 140 minutes and one direct goal involvement each 87.5 minutes. This also means that Cristiano scored four goals and had provided five assists, for nine direct goal involvements in 1184 minutes of appearances at three consecutive major international championships for senior players, comprising 2 consecutive European Championship and 1 FIFA World Cup in which he scored in all three tournaments, at an average of one score every 296 minutes, 1 assist each 236.80 minutes, and one direct goal involvement each 131.56 minutes throughout his significant international tournaments. Cristiano's four goals and three assists in 900 minutes of 10 games for Portugal throughout the season, along with his 40 assists and 42 goals during 4032 minutes over 48 appearances with Manchester United meant he had finished his 2007/08 season of competitive play for both country and club with 13 goals and 46 goals. assists, totalling 59 direct goal involvements in 4932 minutes over the 58 games, which is 1 goal per 107.22 minutes with one assist each 379.38 minutes as well as one goal participation each 83.59 minutes of competitive matches with Manchester United and Portugal. Cristiano's 135 minute playing time in two games for Portugal made his total stats for the year at thirteen assists and 46 goals in 5067 minutes of games with Manchester United and Portugal throughout the entire season.

Cristiano's remarkable performances throughout the 2007/08 season won him a variety of individual accolades at the different levels of Manchester United, the Premier League, English Football to the highest levels of European Football and World Football and he concluded the 2007/08 season with an historic records of 26 individual honours during a single season as the distinction of a

Premier League Player, consisting of The Goal 50 award; spot within the 2007 FIFPro World XI; Champions League Final Fans Man of the Award for Match as well as The Champions Top Goal Scorer honor and The UEFA Best Forward Awards and The UEFA Club Footballer of the Year Awards as well as The European Golden Boot Award; an appearance within the UEFA Team of the Year as well as a spot within the ESM Team of the Season and The CNID The Best Portuguese Athlete Abroad Award; one award in 2008: the EURO Man of the Match Award and The Podium of the France football Ballon d'Or Award; the Onze d'Argent at the Onze Mondial European Footballer of the Year Award and the Podium of the FIFA World Player of the Year Award as well as The Premier League Player of the Season Award and The Premier League Golden Boot Award and two Premier League Player of the Month Awards Two BBC Goal of the Month Awards as well as The FWA footballer of the year Award as well as The PFA Players' Player of the Year Award as well as the PFA Fans Players of the of the Year award; spot on the PFA Team of the Year and The Manchester United Players' Player of the Year Award as well as the Sir Matt Busby Player of the Year Award. The fact that an outstanding player like Cristiano was at that moment within the ranks of the team was a huge honour as he helped lead Manchester United to its best season in more than 10 years during the season 2007-08. He helped the team win three team honours, including the English Premier League title, the 2007 FA Community Shield and the Champions League title, which was the last title that the team has ever won since.

6.9. CRISTIANO RONALDO CONCLUDES his MANCHESTER United Career as the best player in the world As he guides the CLUB to a CLUB WORLD CUP and PREMIER LEAGUE, as well as an EFL CUP TREBLE AND A successful CHAMPIONS LEAGUE FINAL during the 2008/09 season.

The start of the 2008/09 football season, just five days before Manchester United's first preseason game for the season 7 July 2008 Cristiano had surgery to repair an ankle injury that was severe. This injury came as a major setback to the undisputed Top player at the moment in World Football, as it prevented Cristiano to play in the preseason. Moreover, the only time he returned to the field was after two years and 10 weeks on the 17th of September in 2008, and during that the time he missed six games in competition with Manchester United and 3 appearances for Portugal. When Cristiano was recuperating from his ankle injury, the Spanish Club, Real Madrid, was extremely keen to sign the promising young player, who was also keen on shifting towards Madrid, the Spanish Capital. After talks with Team Manager Sir Alex Ferguson, Cristiano accepted to remain for Manchester United, which had lodged a tampering case with FIFA regarding Real Madrid's search for their player, however FIFA the President Sepp Blatter chose to not take any action, simply describing Manchester United's claim to own a player, without being able to leave if he wanted to being modern day slavery a statement which Cristiano was adamant about, nevertheless remained with Manchester United for the season however. Without their top and most innovative player missing, Manchester United struggled in the 2008 FA Community Shield at the Wembley Stadium against Portsmouth on the 10th of August, 2008 after the match was unable to score however, Manchester United managed to win 3-1 in penalties shootout. The victory earned Cristiano the second FA Community Shield honor and the fifth trophy to date in English Football. In the absence of Cristiano, Manchester United started their Premier League title defense with an away draw with Newcastle United on August 17 2008. They then followed that up with a 1-0 home victory against Portsmouth the following day on 25 August the 25th of August, 2008. However, the absence of Cristiano was felt deeply in the Manchester United's UEFA Super Cup 2-1 loss against Russian Europa League Champions, Zenit Saint Petersburg, in Monaco on the 29th of August 2008. Despite having signed the Brazilian twins Fabio and Rafael who are from the Brazilian club Fluminense and Forward Dimitar Berbatov from the same English Premier League side, Tottenham Hotspur, following the departures of Louis Saha, Mikael Silvestre, Chris Eagles, Gerard Pique, Kieran Lee and Dong Fangzhou, Manchester United were still without Cristiano when they lost their Premier League Matchday 3 game at 2-1 to Liverpool on Anfield on September 13 the 13th of September, 2008. This is Manchester United's only Premier League loss against Liverpool in more than 4 years following their April 4, 2004 defeat at the end of Matchday 37 during the 2003/04 campaign. It was also the first time that the Portugal National Team also clearly was missing their captain, since on the 10th of September the 10th of September, 2008 Portugal suffered its loss in their first game in over 4 years, ever since the loss on July 4, 2004, against Greece in Greece's EURO 2004 Final, after an 3-2 loss at home to Denmark at their first game of the 2010 World Cup European Group Qualifier.

On the 17th of September in 2008, after recovering from an injury Cristiano was the first player to start the Manchester United's Champions League title defense on the bench, while they played Spanish team, Villareal, in their Group E opener. But, in the second minute of the game, Cristiano made his long-awaited return from injury to the cheers and applause from the Old Trafford spectators in replacement Park. His appearance and performance prompted the Manchester to take control of the game, although they came close to scoring numerous times, and even hitting posts, the game ended in a draw, which it was the third consecutive draw that was goalless among Manchester United as well as Villareal. The draw meant that Manchester United's streak of twelve consecutive wins at home during the UEFA Champions League was not extended. On the 21st of September in 2008. Cristiano did not start in the Manchester United's Matchday 4 league game at Stamford Bridge against Chelsea, however, he was substituted at the end of 55 minutes in place of Scholes after the match finished 1-1. The 23rd of September, 2008 Cristiano made his debut in the current season with Manchester United after his return from injury during the Manchester United's EFL Cup Third Round match against Middlesbrough at Old Trafford, and inspired his team to victory scoring his very first strike of the year, his 25th minute strike which gave their team a one-goal initial half win , before being replaced in favor of Tevez at the beginning of the 61st second minute, and they ultimately beat 3-1 to make it to the next stage of the tournament. On the 27th of September the 27th of September, 2008 Cristiano made his debut Premier League start in Manchester United's Matchday 5 league game at home against Bolton Wanderers, and after the first period was at 0-0, he provided an insight into the things his team was missing from the Premier League as he struggled to get back to his best and gave Manchester United a 2:2 win by opening scoring and assisting in the at the 60th minute after being fouled by the goalkeeper in the other team's game and converted the penalty. He also provided an outstanding back-heel assistance during the final minute of the match to score the goal that ended the game, only to be substituted by Nani during the 80th minute. Cristiano's remarkable performance was crucial to the faces of the reigning Champions, moving them from 15th place in the league to eighth position , with eight points. The 30th of September, 2008 Cristiano completed the month playing in full-time as Manchester United travelled to Denmark to play Aalborg during their 2nd Champions League Group E match at the Aalborg Portland Park. after his excellent sixth minute ball was mishandled by Berbatov, he gave his assistance for his third strike in the final minutes that resulted in Manchester United a 3-0 victory. Cristiano's assist was his third assist in two games and his fifth direct goal in three consecutive appearances. Cristiano's return from injury were a huge comfort from Manchester United that had been struggling since returning to the club of their star player. Cristiano completed September 2008 with two goals and three assists in 294 minutes of play in two starts in five appearances during the Champions League, the Premier League and the EFL Cup.

Cristiano started the month of October with a full-time appearance in Manchester United's Matchday 6 league game at Ewood Park against Blackburn Rovers on October 4, 2008 and, after helping his team win 1-1 win in the first half and an assist in the pull-back for the final goal of the game to secure the win 2-0 which elevated Manchester United to 6th position in the league standings, with 11 points. In the lead-up to the international break Cristiano's eagerly anticipated return to captain Portugal's National Team for the first time since his appointment as Captain. Portugal National Team for the first time since his appointment as the team's permanent Captain was coming close to a conclusion. Cristiano's first game as permanent captain of Portugal was their third World Cup European Qualifier on the 11th of October on the Rasunda Fotballstadion against Sweden that included such fellow teammates from Cristiano such as Zlatan Ibrahimovic as well as Kim Kallstrom. Captain Cristiano took part in the entire match that ended in a 1-1 draw. A few days later Captain Cristiano took part in the entire match in their fourth World Cup European Qualifier at the Estadio Municipal de Braga against an aggressive Albania who kept Portugal to a goalless draw. On the 18th of October 2008. Cristiano took part in the entire match when Manchester United hosted West Bromwich Albion for their Matchday 7 league game, and scored his 5th consecutive direct goal in four consecutive matches in the match for Manchester United by scoring their second goal using left-footed shots into the legs of the Goalkeeper of their opponent during the final minute of the match in which they prevailed 4-1 to move to fourth in the league, with 14 points. This was their highest point since the beginning of the season, thanks to Cristiano's returning from injury. On the 21st of October of 2008, Cristiano was on the pitch for the entire game in the match as Manchester United hosted Celtic in their third

Champions League Group E game which they defeated the Scottish team 3-0 to move to the first in the group with seven points. The following day, Cristiano played all 90 minutes when Manchester United visited Goodison Park for their Matchday 8 match of the league game against Everton as well as helped lead his team earn an 1-1 draw, which led the team to drop a spot on the league table , and drop to 5th place at 15 points. On the 29th of October of 2008. Cristiano finished the month with a full-time appearance in the Manchester United's Matchday 9 league game at home against West Ham United, and scoring two goals in the first period The first goal was scored with a left-footed strike to at the back of the goal in 14 minutes, and the second goal was scored by a right-footed strike in the 30th minute, which was enough to bring his team to the win 2-0. The goal was his 23rd goal of his career. Despite their win, which brought the number of points they earned in league up to 18 Manchester United went down to sixth place on the table. Cristiano finished the month of October with three goals and one assist, which is 4 goals in five appearances of 450 minutes with Manchester United in the Premier League and the Champions League, and with 180 minutes of playing in two appearances for Portugal.

Cristiano began the month of November by playing in the entire match in which Manchester United hosted Hull City for Matchday 10 of the league on the opening day of November, and he helped his team win victory with an opening goal scored by an unorthodox shot from the 3rd minute. He then scored the final goal of the game by scoring a header in the 44th minute, giving Manchester United a 3-1 first half victory. They eventually beat the opponent 4-3 and moved up to third on the table for the very first time during the current season, with 21 points. Two goals in the game meant Cristiano scored consecutive braces in two consecutive Premier League appearances, and it was his 24th time he had scored a brace in his career, and the fourth time that he scored back-to-back braces. On the 5th of November, the 5th of November, 2008 Cristiano was a full participant in the game as Manchester United travelled to Celtic for their fourth Champions League Group E game in Group E. With the team down by 1-0, he gave the assist via a deft strike from 25 yards which proved too intense for the Celtic goalkeeper to control in the 84th minute, which was their goal to make it 1-1. The goal was enough to earn Manchester United a point from the match , and also kept their winning streak of the Champions League in tact while helping them increase the number of points they have scored to eight in Group E. Furthermore, it was Cristiano's fifth goal-related involvement in three consecutive games for Manchester United. On the 8th of November 2008. Cristiano was present throughout the match when Manchester United visited Arsenal at the Emirates Stadium for Matchday 11 of the league. after his team fell behind 2-0 and 2-0 down, he scored the header to score an equalizer in the 90th minute, as they fell 2-1 and were down to 4th in the league table that would put them in their lowest ranking throughout the remainder this season. This was Cristiano's sixth consecutive direct goal contribution during four consecutive Manchester United appearances. On the 15th of November in 2008, Cristiano was a part of the Manchester United's Matchday 12 league game at home against Stoke City, and inspired his team to victory when he scored the first strike in just the third minutes of the game with a an swerving and dipping free-kick that was his 100th goal in a competitive match in the history of Manchester United and then providing the assist for the subsequent goal in the 45th minute, before scoring the final goal at the end of the 90th minute the fifth goal, thanks to a good free-kick. The home team defeated 5-0 to move up to third in the league, with 24 points. The brace from a free-kick was Cristiano's 25th in his career, which meant the striker had scored three braces in three games within 9 straight direct goal participations in five consecutive appearances with Manchester United. These goals also meant Cristiano had scored impressively against every team who played within the

English Premier League for the 2008/09 season. It was is a remarkable feat in the last year of Premier League football.

On the 20th of November the 20th of November, 2008 Captain Cristiano played for Portugal during an international match match against Brazil which was his first match at a stadium in South America at the Estadio Valmir Campelo Bezerra in Brazil and was a part of all through the game when Portugal was defeated by 6-2. Two days after the game that took place in Brazil, Cristiano was started in Manchester United's Matchday 13 league encounter at Villa Park against Aston Villa however, he was withdrawn in the 82nd minute by Anderson after the match finished with a 0-0 draw. It was the first time Manchester United had failed to score in the course of a Premier League game in since November 24, 2007, due in part to the fact their top player was tired from their long journey between and to Brazil that gave him less than a full day to recuperate and prepare for the match alongside his fellow players against an aggressive Aston Villa side playing in their backyard. But, Manchester United kept their third spot in the league by scoring 25 points. On November 25, the year 2008 Manchester United travelled to the La Ceramica to clash with Villareal in their fifth Champions League Group E game with just one point to qualify for the knockout phase of the tournament. Cristiano was on the pitch for the entire game in the role of Joan Capdevila was deployed to target him with a lot of force after the latter was a victim of several fouls against Cristiano who led to the Portuguese to receive an yellow card for disobedience after protesting against the referee for not penalizing Villareal players for deliberately fouling them, the officials finally issued Capdevila an immediate red card for a serious charge against Cristiano after he engaged in the challenge with raised studs. The game ended in a goalless draw to mark the fourth consecutive draw that was goalless in the match between Manchester United and Villareal, since Manchester United qualified for the Round of 16 in the Champions League with one game to leave. The 30th of November, 2008 Cristiano was the Manchester United's first player to start their final game of the month Their Matchday 14 league game against Manchester City at the City of Manchester Stadium in the very initial Manchester Derby of the season and led his team take an 1-0 lead, before being given another yellow card, and being sent off at the 68th minute. the game ended with the same score and bringing the number of points they scored to 28, and securing their third position at the top of their league. Cristiano completed November 2008 with four goals and 3 assists in 600 minutes over seven games with Manchester United in the Premier League and Champions League, and with an appearance of 90 minutes for Portugal.

Cristiano began the month of December 2008 with the Manchester United's Matchday 15 league game of the season, at home against Sunderland and was then rested to Ryan Giggs in the 67th minute, as they prevailed 1-1 to maintain third in the league, with 31 points. On the 10th December 2008. Cristiano did not play because of his poor performance. Manchester United hosted Aalborg in their final Champions League Group E match and disappointingly they were able to draw 2-2 to win the group, but only because Villareal was defeated by Celtic. Manchester United therefore topped Group E with 12 points and later was played against Jose Mourinho's Inter Milan in the upcoming Champions League Round of 16. The 13th of December, the 13th of December, 2008 Cristiano took part in the entire game as Manchester United visited White Hart Lane for their Matchday 16 game of the Premier League season against Tottenham Hotspur that ended in a draw and maintained their third spot in the league, scoring 32 points. This was the final match for Manchester United prior to their participation in the FIFA Club World Cup, against the champions of continental clubs of FIFA's constituting continental football federations, in the Semifinal , in which Manchester United were in the semi-final. Red Devils had qualified by due to their success as champions of 2007/08's UEFA Champions League season, since they are the UEFA Champions League Club Champions generally qualify directly for the Semifinals, similar to they do for the CONMEBOL Copa Libertadores Club Champions. On the 18th of December 18, 2008, Cristiano was the first player to make the FIFA Club World debut by playing all of Manchester United's Semifinal match in this year's edition of the tournament in the International Stadium of Yokohama against Japanese team along with AFC Champions League winners, Gamba Osaka. They achieved the game's second goal game with a 45th minute header with a score of 5-3 in order to secure their spot in the final.

This year's FIFA Club World Cup Final took place on the 21st of December in 2008 at the International Stadium of Yokohama between Manchester United and Ecuadorian side and CONMEBOL Copa Libertadores Champions, LDU Quito. Cristiano was in the entire match and, after Manchester United had gone down to 10 men following Vidic received a red card for his violent conduct as a big Game player, Cristiano inspired his team to victory by grabbing an unmarked ball near one of the edges of the penalty zone and then delivering an assist that won the match for Rooney who scored the winning goal at the end of the third minute. Cristiano's contribution to the game assisted Manchester United to win its First Ever FIFA Club World Cup. The assist that won the game demonstrated Cristiano's ability to create the significant difference in tough and important matches by direct involvement in goals and outstanding displays which Manchester United had clearly missed in its UEFA Super Cup loss without his assistance at the beginning this season. With his impressive performances and 2 consecutive goals during two games, which included the goal and assists, Cristiano won the Silver Ball Award as the 2nd Most Valuable Player at the FIFA Club World Cup. It was a huge honor for him. FIFA Club World Cup win signified that Cristiano was a catalyst for Manchester United to victory in at least one round of every tournament he played in with the club including his participation in the FA Cup, the EFL Cup and the FA Community Shield, the Premier League and the UEFA Champions to the FIFA Club World Cup, by his exceptional performances in these tournaments which earned him scores of individual honours. On the 26th of December of 2008. Cristiano was the first player to play in a match following having had his FIFA Club World Cup exploits and helped his team to win a full game performance to a 1-0 win against Stoke City at the Britannia Stadium in their 17th game of the season in league, in which they maintained their third spot in the league, with 35 points. On December 29 of 2008, Cristiano ended the year with playing with the team as Manchester United hosted Middlesbrough in their 18th league match of the season. having helped his squad take an 1-0 lead after which he was substituted for Giggs during the final minute of the match, as they beat Middlesbrough by the same score to finish the season at third place, in the league with 38 points. Cristiano completed December 2008 with one goal and one assist in 511 minutes over 6 games with Manchester United in the Premier League as well as the 2009 FIFA Club World Cup.

Cristiano finished 2008 with 14 assists. This translates into 48 direct goals in 50 appearances with Manchester United for an average of one goal every 121.09 minutes and 1 assist per 294.07 minutes with one involvement in a direct goal every 85.77 minutes. Alongside his one goal and three assists in five games with Portugal, Cristiano ended 2008 with 17 goals and 35 assists. This totals 52 direct goals in 4567 minutes of 58 appearances , for an average of one goal per 130.49 minutes, one assists each 268.65 minutes and a direct goal participation every 87.83 minutes during competitive games with Manchester United and Portugal. Along with his 225 minutes played in three friendlies, Cristiano ended 2008 with 17 assists and 35 goals in 4820 minutes over his 61 appearances with the national and club. In 2008, even with two months of injuries, Cristiano won the FIFA World Player of the

Year Award for the first time in his professional career. He also won the most recent version of the FIFPro World Player of the Year Award and became the only third player to receive the award following Brazilians, Ronaldinho and Kaka. He was included as part of the 2009 FIFPro World XI , as being among the three most effective forwards within World Football, which made him the only and first Ever player to make it into the elite team in two different positions. He played at the time of the previous edition in the midfielder position. He was also the first player to win the award in consecutive seasons. Cristiano was awarded the France Football Ballon d'Or Award for the first time in his professional career. He also received the World Soccer World Player of the Year Award for the first time in his career. He also won the Onze d'Or Award for the first time in his career following having won the second-place Onze d'Argent award the year before.

Cristiano was named for the third and the for the second time in his career , in the UEFA Team of the Year in 2008 being named one of the Top three Midfielders from European Football, as he was a highly efficient goal-scoring Wing Midfielder who was viewed as a Forward because he scored goals just like a regular Forward. He did this prior to his transition to a Wing forward after his move from Real Madrid. Cristiano received an additional two consecutive CNID the Best Portuguese Athlete in the United States Award for the year 2008. Cristiano's individual awards at the end of the year along with the Club World Cup Silver Ball Award elevated his honours since the beginning of the season to 9 that includes his two Premier League Player of the Month Awards as well as two BBC Goal of the Month Awards as well as His 2007/08 Champions League Final Fans' Man of the Match Award and Champions League Top Goal Scorer award as well as His 2007/08 English Football Premier League Golden Boot, Premier League Player of the Season, the FWA Footballer of the Year, the PFA Players'

Player of the Year and PFA Fans Player of the Year Awards and inclusion on the PFA Team of the Year and the ESM Team of the Season as well as the 2007/08 European Golden Shoe, UEFA Best Player of the Year and UEFA Best Forward of the Year Awards as well as The Goal 50 Award; 3 Manchester United season-end Player of the Year Awards as well as the EURO 2008 Man of the Award. This brought his total annual honors to an amazing and historic record of 30 for the record of a Premier League Player. The total of 30 individual awards during the year of Cristiano was unprecedented , and nobody before him , or in the past, has achieved this level of accomplishment in an entire season in English Football. Cristiano completed 2008 with four honours as a team player, which included: the English Premier League, the UEFA Champions League, the FIFA Club World Cup and the FA Community Shield. In the course of the year, Cristiano was awarded damages for Libel lawsuits and gave the proceeds to a charitable organization in Madeira. Cristiano was the main character of the 2007's Pro Evolution

Soccer, as was also featured as the front cover for the game's video for the 2011 and 2013 versions.

Cristiano started January 2009 with a came on as an emergency 63rd-minute substitution to Paul Scholes in Manchester United's January 7th, 2009 trip the Derby County's Pride Park Stadium for the first leg of the EFL Cup Semifinal tie with his team trailing by 1-0 against the Championship team due to Sir Alex Ferguson's plan prior to the match to not rest him, but Manchester United fought hard to take the lead and win the game by 1-0. On January 11 the 11th of January 2009 Cristiano was the first player to play a full game of the season when Manchester United hosted Chelsea in their 19th league match of the season. even though his goal in the 45th minute not being allowed, he gave an assist from a free kick for his team's third strike in the final minute of the game, as they prevailed 3-0 to keep third place having 41 points. The following day, Cristiano played the whole game as Manchester United hosted

Wigan Athletic in their 20th league match and he scored another consecutive goal to the first goal, and eventually goal-winner at the 56th second of the game. The 1-0 win moved Manchester United up to second position on the ladder for only the second time during the season , and they scored 44 points. On the 17th of January 2009 Cristiano was on the pitch for all of 90 minutes, and helped lead his team score the 1-0 victory against Bolton Wanderers at the Macron Stadium in their 21st league match, in which they finished top of League for just the third time during the entire season, scoring 47 points and held this position until the end of the season. On the 20th of January 2009 Cristiano did not start in the second leg of Manchester United's EFL Cup Semifinal against Derby County at Old Trafford, but came in at 58 minutes to allow Giggs scoring Manchester United's vital tie-winner in the 87th minute with a penalty, which earned the team a win of 4-2 and a score of 4-3 which allowed him to play in the second EFL Cup Final. Cristiano's goal was particularly important since a win of 3-2 could have taken Derby County to the Final due to an away-goal rule. On the 24th of January 2009 Cristiano began the Manchester United's FA Cup Round of 16 match in the home of Tottenham Hotspur, and after aiding his team to the lead of 2-1 the team was substituted in the 72nd minute by Zoran Tosic. The match finished with the same scoreline , which helped allow the hosts to progress to the Quarterfinals of the tournament. Cristiano took part in the entire the Manchester United Matchday 22 league game at The Hawthorns Stadium against West Bromwich Albion on the 27th of January, 2008 and scored the fifth and fourth goals of the game with left-footed strikes in the 65th and 73rd minute when they beat West Bromwich Albion 5-0 and kept them at the top of their league. Red Devils top of the league with 50 points. This was his 26th goal goal of Cristiano's career. Clean sheets set two Premier League records that Cristiano was able to achieve through his defensive contribution including the longest consecutive clean sheets during the course of a Premier

League season (11) and the longest amount of time played by a Goalkeeper the Premier League without conceding a goal to Edwin van der Saar with 1,032 minutes. On the 31st of January in the 2008 season, Cristiano finished the year with a full game in which Manchester United hosted Everton in their 23rd league game and scoring the only goal of the match with an injury in the 44th minute to keep their top spot in the league, with 53 points. Cristiano completed January 2009 with four goals and two assists in 581 minutes of playing with Manchester United.

Cristiano started February 2009 by becoming 24 years old on the 5th of February the 5th of February 2009. On February 8 the 8th of February 2009, Cristiano played the full game as Manchester United visited West Ham United at the Boleyn Ground for their 24th league match of the season. During which , despite not being awarded the chance to score a penalty following a tripping during the final minutes of the match he nevertheless helped the team to win by 1-0. The victory brought end the host's six-game undefeated streak prior to the match and also kept them at the top of the league, with 56 points. A few days later during the international break Captain Cristiano took part in the entire game and scored the sole goal of the game during the game. Portugal defeated Finland 1-1 in a friendly international at the Estadio Algarve. Cristiano scored his first goal in just four games after his appointment to the position of permanent Capt for Portugal's national team. Portugal National Team, and this victory was also his first win as the permanent captain. In February of 2009 Cristiano began the game as Manchester United visited Pride Park to play the FA Cup Round of 16 game against Derby County, which was the third Cup match between the two teams in 39 days. He provided the assist to the second goal of the game at the end of 44 minutes, before scoring the third goal in the 68th minute, before being substituted for Possebon at the 72nd moment, as the home team defeated 4-1 to make it into the quarterfinals. On February 18 2009 Cristiano took part in the entire game as Manchester United hosted Fulham in their 25th league match of the season. He was instrumental in helping his team win an 3-0 win that earned them a five-point advantage at leading the Premier League table, with 59 points. A clean sheet meant that Manchester United had extended their Premier League clean sheets record to 14 consecutive games as well. van der Sar had also increased his record in the Premier League of the most consecutive minutes played without conceding an score to 1302 minutes. A few days later, Cristiano played the entire game as a rotating Manchester United side hosted Blackburn Rovers in their 26th league game and was able to help his team take a an 1-0 advantage that lasted for 9 minutes, when Blackburn Rovers equalized to set the record for Continuous Minutes without conceding goals within the English Premier League to be recorded at 1334 minutes after which he scored an amazing free-kick that was shot from a small angle towards the right of the penalty box at the end of 60 minutes, to bring his team to a 1-1 win, which kept the top spot in the league with the score of 62 points. On February 24, 2009 Cristiano finished the month by playing all the way through the game in the midst of a trip to Italy. Manchester United travelled to Italy to play Inter Milan at the Stadio San Siro-Guiseppe meazza for the first leg in their Champions Round of 16 match and helped the team draw 0-0. Cristiano completed the month with two goals and 1 assist over 432 minutes during five matches with Manchester United in the Premier League and in the FA Cup and the Champions League as well as a goal in his 90 minutes for Portugal.

Cristiano began the month of March 2009 with a full game of the EFL Cup Final against Tottenham Hotspur at Wembley on the 1st of March 2009, and the game finished with a 0-0 draw after 90 minutes, at the end of the stoppage time, the game, he hit into the interior of the post , but it didn't go in. Extra time was also with no goals and the winner had to be determined by the penalty shootout, which was only two times during EFL Cup Final history. The shootout result was 1-1, Cristiano scored his penalty to give Manchester United a 3-1 lead after David Bentley missed for Tottenham and Anderson scored the second in the favor of Manchester United to win their third EFL Cup trophy. It was the EFL Cup Final was the second one that Cristiano was part of and was crowned. Just three hours after winning their EFL Cup triumph, Manchester United came to St. James' Park for their 27th league match in the league against Newcastle United with van der Sar returning to the team after being absent for the previous two English Football matches, but was unable to add 9 minutes in his time which was 1311. Premier League Minutes without Conceding the goal, as he conceded the opening goal in the match. Cristiano was on the pitch for the entire game and guided his team achieve a 3-1 comeback victory, which kept Manchester United top of the league with 65 points. On March 11 2009 Cristiano took part in the entire game as Manchester United hosted Inter Milan in the second leg in their Champions League Round of 16 match. Despite being aware it was the case that Manchester United under Sir Alex Ferguson had defeated teams managed under Jose Mourinho only once in the previous 13 meetings, Cristiano scored the second and final goal in the match to secure the hosts the victory, which ensured their place into the Champions League Quarterfinals. A few days later, Cristiano played the entire game as Manchester United hosted Liverpool in their 28th league match of the season. And despite scoring the opening goal with an injury in the 23rd minute, Vidic was sent off after the hosts fell 4-1 but held their position as the first team at the top of their league. Cristiano took part in the entire game of the Manchester United's 29th league match in the league in Craven Cottage against Fulham on March 21, 2009 when the two players Scholes and Rooney received red cards . Ultimately, the hosts were defeated two-to-two, but they did manage to finish at the top in the table. The two consecutive league defeats occurred for the first time in the season 2004/05 when

Manchester United had lost 2 consecutive Premier League matches since at Norwich City on April 9 in 2005, followed by Everton in April the same year. The international break ended on the 28th of March 2009, during a full match appearance Captain Cristiano was able to lead Portugal to an 0-0 draw with Sweden for their sixth match of the 2010 World Cup European Qualifier at the Estadio do Dragao. The 31st of March 2009 Captain Cristiano completed the month with making his debut at the end of the second half in the 57th minutes to replace Nani in an international friendly match against South Africa at the Stade Olympique de la Pontaise, and assisting Portugal to win 2-0. Cristiano finished March 2009 with two goals in 480 minutes of 5 appearances with Manchester United in the Premier League, EFL Cup Final and Champions League, and with the score of 153 minutes over two games for Portugal.

Cristiano began the month of April 2009 by playing all the way through the game and guiding Manchester United to a much-needed home win over Aston Villa in their 30th league match that season, on April 5 after scoring the opening goal of the game with a free-kick that was direct at the end of 13 minutes and when the opposition scored two goals, he responded by scoring their third strike in the 80th minute , to draw level with a right-footed strike that prompted debutant Federico Macheda, to score the game-winning goal in the 90th minute +3 minutes, to allow Manchester United to maintain its top spot in the table of league positions with an impressive 68 points. The goal was the 27th goal Cristiano has scored in his career. Just two days later, Cristiano played the full match when Manchester United hosted FC Porto in the first Leg in their Champions League Quarterfinal tie, and helped his team win an 2-2 draw. The 11th of April, 2009 Cristiano began Manchester United's final league fixture in the league with Sunderland on the Stadium of Light, and played his part in an early 1-0 victory and was then removed in the 69th minute for Park who won 2-1 to remain top of the league with 70 points. On the 15th of April of 2009 Cristiano took part in the entire match . Manchester United travelled to the Estadio do Dragao to clash against FC Porto in the Second Phase in their Champions League Quarterfinal tie, and was the only player who helped his team advance into finals of the Champions League Semifinals by scoring the sole goal of the game by launching an amazing long distance shot from 40 yards away at the end of 6 minutes. It was able to fly past the Porto Goalkeeper and into the upper corner. Because of his incredible shot, Manchester United became the first Ever English team to beat FC Porto at the Estadio do Dragao and the aggregate victory of 3-2 pushed Manchester United into a third consecutive Champions League Semifinal. Cristiano's incredible and stunning goal was the inspiration behind the development of the FIFA Puskas Award for the most outstanding Goal of World Football and it enabled him to win the first edition at the conclusion of the year. It it also earned him the Manchester United Goal of the Season Award for 2008/09.

The next day and without Cristiano, Manchester United was eliminated in the semi-finals at home of the FA Cup by Everton through an edgy penalty shootout that ended with a score of 4-2. In April of 2009 Cristiano took part in the entire match of the Manchester United 32nd league game that season, against Portsmouth and was able to help his team win 2 - 0 home victory that kept the team in the top position in the league, scoring the score of 74 points. On April 25 2009 Cristiano was a full participant in the match of the 33rd League match of the season , at their home stadium against Tottenham Hotspur, and after they lost the opening half by 2-0, he helped his team win an 5-2 win by kicking off their scoring with an injury time penalty in the 56th minute, later scoring the crucial third goal with an 68th minute header, and then assisting for the 4th goal in the game at the end of the first minute. It was the second goal goal of Cristiano's career. The victory put Manchester United 3 points clear on top of the league table, with 77 points. On the 29th of April

2009, Cristiano ended the month by playing in the entire game as Manchester United hosted Arsenal in the first Leg in their Champions League Semifinal tie, and was on top form to lead the team score a 1-1 win. Cristiano finished the month with five goals and one assist in 609 minutes of play in seven appearances with Manchester United in the Premier League as well as in the Champions League.

Cristiano began in the 5th month 2009 on May 5, 2009, playing the entire duration of the second leg of Manchester United's Champions League Semifinal against Arsenal at the Emirates Stadium, and put on an impressive performance that helped to qualify Manchester United to a second consecutive Champions League Final with the 4-1 aggregate win. he was the one to assist the opening score in the eighth minute. He scoring the second goal with an incredible free-kick, which was about 35 yards during the 11th minutes and scored their third goal of the game with an 61st minute right-footed strike to secure victory by 3-1 after an unpopular red card to Darren Fletcher that made him not available for the Final lead to a penalty goal by the hosts. The goal was his 29th of the career. Manchester United's progression to the Final was one of the teams that has not been there since Juventus back in 1997, to make the Champions League Final after winning the tournament in the previous year, and also the first team to make it to consecutive Finals for eight years, as Valencia did it in 2001. On the 10th of May the 10th of May 2009 Cristiano began Manchester United's league 35 game when they played their city opponents, Manchester City, and despite leading his team to victory with an unintentional free-kick in the 17th minute from 25 yards and leading his team win 2-0 in the first-half win however, he was replaced at 58 minutes, which was not a happy moment for the player who was replaced as the game ended with the same score to keep the hosts in their highest position in the league, with the score of 83 points. On May 13th, 2009 Cristiano took part in the entire the 36th league match in the league away from Wigan Athletic, and helped his team win victory of 2-1 that raised their point total to the highest of the league standings by 85. In May 16th, 2009 Cristiano took part in the entire match in the match as Manchester United hosted Arsenal for their 37th game of the season. just needing one drawing to be crowned league champions and when a goal the player assisted was disallowed, the game was without a goal to allow Manchester United to win their third consecutive English Premier League title and 18th English Championships overall. The third consecutive Cristiano-powered Premier League title made Manchester United the first Ever team to be the winners of this Premier League 3 times consecutively twice, and also do the similar in the 1998/99 and 2000/2001 seasons.

On the 24th of May in 2009 Cristiano did not play as a substitute. Manchester United side beat Hull City in a 1-0 win to complete the Premier League season as Champions for the third consecutive year with the best 90 points since the arrival of Cristiano. Despite suffering from a two-month injury in the first half of the season Cristiano completed with the Premier League season as Manchester United's top goal scorer with 18 goals. He was also the Second Most Assists Provider, having 8 assists just behind Dimitar Berbatov's 9 assists and the most direct Goal Involvements with 26 direct involvements in goals in Manchester United's league, which was tied for with the second highest 68 goals in the duration of 2743 minutes across 33 games which means he had played in 41.18 percent in Manchester United's League goals throughout the season. He averaged 1 goal per 152.39 minutes, 1 assist each 342.88 minutes, and one direct goal each 105.50 minutes played by Manchester United in the English Premier League season. Cristiano is the premier league's Direct Goal Involvements Player with 26 goals; the Second Top Goal Scorer, with only one goal less as Nicholas Anelka with 19 goals as well as Third Top Assists Provider with eight assists along with Ashley Young, Cesc Fabregas,

Steed Malbranque, Steven Pienaar and Dirk Kuyt, after Frank Lampard and Robin van Persie with 10 assists each as well as Berbatov, Steven Ireland, James Milner and Steven Gerrard with nine assists each. Even though Cristiano being the best player both in Manchester United, the English Premier League and English Football throughout the 2008/09 season, his outstanding performances were only recognized through his fourth appearance in the PFA Premier League Team of the Year. One thinks it was due to his imminent departure of Manchester United and English Football or if it was due to the fact that he was the winner of almost every season-end award the two previous seasons, none of which are related to merit.

On May 27, 2009 Cristiano finished the final chapter of his Manchester United career by playing the entire duration of 2008/09's UEFA Champions League Final at the Stadio Olimpico di Roma, which Manchester United fell 2-0 to the Barcelona team that included highly talented players such as midfield geniuses and EURO 2008 Champions: Xavi and Iniesta who were the assists on both goals; and forwards: Samuel Eto'o who scored the first goal, Messi who scored the second goal, and Thierry Henry. Cristiano's second place finish at the Champions League was the third honour given to the team in the season 2008/09. Cristiano finished the season in May 2009 with three goals and one assist in 418 minutes during his five Final appearances at Manchester United in the Premier League and the Champions League Final. Cristiano has therefore concluded his last season at Manchester United, the 2008/09 season, despite suffering a two months of injury before the start of the season. He had eight assists and 18 goals over 2743 minutes of 33 Premier League appearances; 4 goals and 3 assists in 1018 minutes over the 12 Champions League appearances; 1 goal and an assist in 180 minutes of two FIFA Club World Cup appearances two goals over the 240-minute period in four EFL Cup appearances; and 1 goal and an assist in two FA Cup appearances; for the total of thirteen assists, and 26 goals, which equates to 39 direct goals in 53 games with Manchester United, meaning he scored an average of one goal per 166.35 minutes; one assists every 332.69 minutes, and one direct goal participation each 110.9 minutes during the 2008/09 season at Manchester United. After the season was over, Cristiano concluded his season by playing in the entire game as Captain Cristiano who led Portugal into a decisive 2-1 victory against Albania at their six-game World Cup Qualifier away at the Selman Stermasi Stadium in Tirana. Captain Cristiano finished his international competitive year with 360 minutes of four matches for Portugal.

Cristiano's competitive international football performance during the season, and his club's performance throughout the entire season brought his overall competitive stats for the country and club through the entire season to the tune of 26 goals, and 13 assists, for an overall total of 39 direct goal participations over 4685 minutes of his 57 appearances. This means that the average was 1-goal every 180.19 minutes, and 1 assist each 360.38 minutes, and one direct goal-related involvement each 120.13 minutes during competitive games in the games of Manchester United and Portugal throughout the season of 2008/09. The goal he scored in 237 minutes of three international matches and Portugal appearances meant that he finished this season on a high with 27 goals, and 13 assists in 4922 minutes of appearances with Manchester United and Portugal. Cristiano's appearance on the PFA Team of the Year as well as the Manchester United Goal of the Season Award, in addition to his nine individual awards at the midseason stage made it possible for him to finish the 2008/09 season with 11 personal awards. The 2009 Laureus World Award for Sportsman of the Year to the most outstanding male athlete of 2008. Cristiano Ronaldo was one of six candidates in this Award to the very first time during his professional career and was crowned by Usain Bolt. Bolt has been awestruck by the power of Cristiano's speed and his sprinting on the football field and said that Cristiano Ronaldo could be the sole footballer with the potential to intimidate him in the track and field. Cristiano was also a key player and the best in Manchester United. Manchester United Team that was nominated for the 2009 Laureus World Sports Award for Team of the Year, which was one of the top teams in world sports during the year in 2008. In terms of team honours, Cristiano concluded his 2008/09 season by winning four times, which included The 2009 FA Community Shield; the EFL Cup; the Premier League and the Champions League Second Place.

Cristiano finished the span of his Manchester United career with the following stats of 51 assists and 84 goals to total 135 direct goal involvements in an average of 14541 minutes during 196 games within the English Premier League, meaning that he averaged one goal per 173.11 minutes, an assistance for every 285.12 minutes. He also had one direct goal participation each 107.71 minutes during your

English Premier League career; 13 assists and 16 goals totalling 30 direct goals in 4421 minutes during 59 games of the UEFA Champions League, meaning that he scored 1.01 goals every 276.31 minutes, one assists per 340.08 minutes. He also had one direct goal involvement each 152.45 minutes during the course of his Champions League career as a Manchester United player; 13 goals and 11 assists, for 24 direct goal participations over 2074 minutes of 26 games at the FA Cup, meaning he averaged one score each 159.54 minutes, and 1 assists for every 188.55 minutes and one direct goal involvement each 86.42 minutes during the course of his FA Cup career; 4 goals and 2 assists , for an overall six direct goal involvements in 930 minutes over 12 games in the EFL Cup, meaning he averaged 1 goal every 218.25 minutes, one assists each 436.5 minutes. He also had one Direct Goal Involvement every 145.5 minutes during the course of his EFL Cup career; 1 goal and one assist to total two direct goal involvements in the course of 180 minutes during two appearances during the FIFA Club

World Cup, which means he averaged one direct goal involvement for each match of the tournament; and only a 90-minute appearance for the FA Community Shield. The overall performance of Cristiano's life in his time as an Manchester United player consisted of 118 goals and 78 assists. This equates to an overall of 196 direct goals in the 22236 minutes of his 296 appearances which means he averaged the equivalent of 1 goal each 188.44 minutes, one assistance every 285.08 minutes and one direct goal involvement each 113.45 minutes during the course of his Manchester United career in the English Premier League, the UEFA Champions League, the FIFA Club World Cup, the FA Cup, the EFL Cup and the FA Community Shield.

In his six years as an Manchester United player, he received every major award and distinction at the levels of Manchester United, English Football, European Football, and World Football, as well being awarded a few awards on the field of International Football due to his exceptional performances in

Portugal. Cristiano's 57 individual accolades over his six seasons as an Manchester United Player consisted of four PFA Premier League Team of the Year appearances as well as four Premier League Player of the Month Awards as well as three UEFA Team of the Year Appearances; 3 Sir Matthew Busby Player of the Year Awards 2. Manchester United Players' Player of the Year Awards and two FIFPro World XI appearances; 2. Premier League Player of the Season Awards 2. FWA Footballer of the Year Awards and 2 PFA Players' Player of the Award 2. PFA fans' Player of the year Awards 2. CNID The Best Portuguese athlete abroad awards two BBC Goal of the Month Awards and 2 FIFPro Extra Youth Player of the Award of the Year 1. FIFA Club World Cup Silver Ball Award; 1 FIFA World Player of the Year Award and One FIFPro World Player of the Year Award and 1. Ballon D'Or Award; 1 Goal 50 Award One World Soccer World Player of the Year Award One Onze d'Or Award and 1. Onze d'Argent Award One UEFA Best Player of the Year Award 1. UEFA Best Forward of the Year

Award and 1. UEFA Champions League Top Goal Scorer Distinction European Golden Shoe Award; 1 Champions League Final Fans' Man of the Match Award One Bravo Award; 1 English Premier League Golden Boot Award; 1 PFA Young Player of the Year Award 1. Manchester United Goal of the Season Award One Manchester United Player of the Year Award which was decided by Manchester United Supporters Club-Cyprus; 1 Second place in the Ballon d'Or Podium 1st place on the FIFA World Player of the Year Podium 1. FA Cup Top Goal Scorer Distinction Two ESM Team of the Season appearances as well as one UEFA EURO Team of the tournament appearance; and one UEFA EURO Player of the match Award. The span of the course of his Manchester United career, Cristiano was awarded 12 team honours at the club. These included 3 English Premier League titles, 2 EFL Cups, 2 FA Community Shields as well as one UEFA Champions League, 1 FIFA Club World Cup, 1 FA Cup, 1 FA Cup Second Place in addition to the UEFA Champions League Second Place. In addition to his two

International Football team honors: 1 UEFA EURO Second Place and 1 FIFA World Cup Fourth Place, Cristiano attained 16 major team awards for the team and country in his time as an Manchester United Player. Cristiano also took home in the friendlies of the Amsterdam Tournament with Manchester United to bring his honours with Manchester United in both official and unofficial tournaments to thirteen. Cristiano's penalty shootout goals of 1 at one FA Cup Final and 1 penalty shootout goal in 1 EFL Cup Final, in addition to the 12 goals he scored in friendly matches for Manchester United meant he had scored 14 goals that were not official in his time as the Manchester United player, hence in official friendly, penalty shootout and official matches, Cristiano was able to score 132 goals in the game for Manchester United in official and non-official matches, and penalty shootouts.

But, prior to his debut game with Real Madrid on July 20 the 20th, he planned to travel into Las Vegas in the United States of America early in July to mark the positive change along with his brother-in-law and cousin. They booked an apartment in an hotel, and on June 12, 2009 Cristiano went out for an enjoyable evening at a bar. He ended up in a club in which a particular Kathryn Mayorga, a budding model who was just a an older year than him, was working to attract wealthy potential clients into the club, and then accompanying them when they got into. In the course of that evening, Cristiano found himself being in the company of a woman who was in awe of him, chatting with him, and remained by his side throughout the night since camera footage of the nightclub have been been revealed. The winner of the Gay Times Sexiest Man Alive Award as well as being one of the most attractive, sexiest and most famous and wealthy people in the world and also the most expensive footballer ever in history of football during the time following his well-publicized record-breaking of his transfer of Manchester United to Real Madrid, Cristiano was every girl's ideal man. Mayorga's behavior demonstrated how fortunate she was about the fantastic opportunity she'd discovered and could be a huge success and boost her modeling career if she was able to be his girlfriend or even make a fortune when she shrewdly planned. After Cristiano left the club Mayorga along with a few colleagues who were happy that Cristiano was providing a wonderful evening were able to follow him to his home where his brother-in-law and his cousin were. While the rest of the group was enjoying themselves in the living space, Mayorga followed Cristiano to his bedroom, without being coerced or compelled. They had a sex session that was consensual which none of the people who were in the room during the time have ever claimed to have used violence or force. The woman eventually left the apartment at around 6:00 am on July 13th, 2009. Cristiano was also able in order to rejoin his former team before his first game with Real Madrid on July 20 in 2009.

In the meantime, Cristiano was looking for only one night with his girlfriend, He didn't realize the fact that Mayorga was looking for more than that. After failing to secure the man to her, Mayorga was left only with the possibility of making some money from him. After leaving the hotel where Cristiano was staying and never revealing the events that transpired from then until the time of 14:00 in the afternoon that day and at the least 11 hours later when she contacted police at the Las Vegas Metropolitan Police Department at her residence to report that she was raped from an athlete. The police were there quickly and tried to get details about the person she was accusing and the location the alleged assault took place but she was unable to divulge the necessary information. But, considering that she was covered in marks that have never disclosed how she fabricated the images, given that no one has ever admitted the fact that she left from the apartment of Cristiano at the hotel. The police brought her to a medical center which a medical professional confirmed the strange marks that she may have been assaulted during the past 12 hours. Cristiano's DNA was evidently discovered on the underwear she wore the night before that she had brought with her. Based on the report of the doctor and the complaint she submitted, without naming the person she was blaming, the police launched investigations into the incident. Then she hired attorneys and later provided Cristiano's name along with the hotels they were associated with that night. The police visited both hotels and spoke with people who were present at their two guests on that evening, including staff members and the colleagues who had taken her to the residence of Cristiano. Because the police couldn't discover any evidence from the United States that linked Cristiano to the allegations that she was claiming and contacted the lawyer for Cristiano in Portugal who was the first to told him about the charges against him. Cristiano was stunned, but he was forced to engage lawyers in his home country of the United States to represent him. Through his lawyer, Cristiano, his cousin and brother-in-law were each provided with questionnaires that they had to complete and returned along with Cristiano sending an oblique sample of his DNA fully in cooperation with the authorities in order to erase his name.

When an investigation by the Las Vegas Metropolitan Police Department took into account all the data they had collected and found no evidence to suggest that Cristiano was assaulting her during their one-night romantic affair. The DNA sample proved that they did have sexual relations, but given the length of time it took her to notify her in order to the police, the absence of witnesses who could verify the marks she left visible on her prior to her departure from the house, the statements from each Cristiano and his family members who claimed to the fact that there were no marks left on her after she left the house and the reality that both were able to enter the bedroom to have the purpose of having a sexual encounter There was no evidence to suggest that Cristiano was guilty of anything, or even raped her or compel her to perform any act, and in the end the investigation was concluded. But realizing that the only thing she and her attorneys were required done to keep Cristiano in a precarious position was keep the matter open before the courtroom, they decided to keep it open it until a judge eventually ordered both parties to begin a contemplated negotiation to settle their disagreements. Cristiano agreed with his lawyers to sign an Non-Disclosure Agreement that would get her the money she needed and shield his name from unscrupulous organizations that could make up the false accusation and then make it appear as if he committed a crime, but there was absolutely no evidence to prove the unsubstantiated claim. It was in the midst of this scandal that Cristiano began with his Real Madrid career. Despite the incident preventing Cristiano from focusing fully on his work and causing him to be injured in the early stages of his time at the newly formed club, he performed very well in the midst of waiting for negotiations to be fruitful. The incident has taught Cristiano an important lesson on certain kind of women who preyed upon young, adventurous men and how innocent one-night flings can end up being costly and destructive.

7.0. The PROFESSIONAL CAREER of CRISTIANO RONDOLDO as a MADRID REAL PLAYER and as CAPTAIN of the PORTUGAL SENIOR National TEAM

7.1. CRISTIANO RONALDO is THE MOST effective footballer in the SPANISH LA LIGA and the CHAMPIONS LEAGUE and EUROPEAN FOOTBALL IN HIS first season as a Real Madrid Player During the 2009/10 season.

The 1st July of 2009, while searching for a new challenge another environment, Cristiano signed a contract with Spanish club, Real Madrid, for the World Record EUR94 million, which ended his glittering Manchester United career and opened new opportunities for him with Real Madrid. The Cristiano Real Madrid contract ran until 2015 and offered him an annual salary of EUR11 million annually. More than 80,000 people were present at Cristiano's debut ceremony on the Real Madrid's Santiago Bernabeu Stadium. The 80,000 or so fans who were present presented Cristiano Ronaldo yet another World Record for the Most Attended Football Player Presentation in the past, surpassing the previous record of 75,000 people who been present for Diego Maradona at Napoli 25 years earlier, and he was already breaking records set by legendary footballers prior to making his debut with Real Madrid. In the 2009/10 season Cristiano's team-mates in Real Madrid were: fellow newcomers Kaka of AC Milan; Xabi Alonso and Alvaro Arbeloa from Liverpool; Karim Benzema from Lyon; Raul Albiol from Valencia; Esteban Granero from Getafe and Ezequiel Garay returning from a loan with Racing Santander; his preseason teammates of the Dutch trio consisting of Arjen Robben who went to Bayern Munich, Wesley Sneijder who was a part of Inter Milan, and Klaas-Jan Huntelaar who went to AC Milan; as well as Fabio Cannavaro who was a part of Juventus;

and helped lead Portugal towards a one-goal victory against Hungary in the Ferenc Puskas Stadion during the eighth World Cup European Qualifier. Cristiano did not start in the Real Madrid's Matchday 2 game of La Liga at the Estadi Cornella-El Prat against Espanyol on September 12, 2009 but he came on at the 65th minute in place of Benzema as he scored the final goal of the game during the 90th minute with a right-footed strike winning 3-0. On the 15th of September in 2009 Cristiano was able to make the Champions League debut by playing the entire game. Real Madrid travelled to the Letzigrund Stadium in Switzerland for their 2009/10 Champions League Group C opener against Zurich He led his team to victory of 5-2 through an unintentional free-kick in the 27th minute and then closing the scoring in that game for a big Game player by completing his free-kicks direct by scoring a 90th+4 minute direct free-kick, which was the 30th goal in his professional career. It was a stunning manner that Cristiano Ronaldo began the course of his Champions League career with Real Madrid in the club that established his name in the role of being known as an Greatest Ever Player to ever take part in the tournament. He would further cement his status as not just an Ultimate Footballer of the History of football and also the Ultimate Big Game Player, and bolstering his right to claim the supreme tradition that was left by being the Greatest Ever player to grace the field and a legacy that that he would build upon following his remarkable consistency in performances throughout the time he was in the team.

On the 20th of September on the 20th of September the year 2009 began, Cristiano began Real Madrid's Matchday 3 La Liga game at home against Xerex and led the team with a 5-1 win after scoring the first goal by scoring a right-footed 1st minute shot. He then, on his own, doubled their lead by scoring an unintentional shot at the end of 75 minutes prior to going off to be replaced by van Nistelrooy in the 79th minute. The score was 3-0. The brace was his 31st of the career. The next day, Cristiano played the entire game when Real Madrid visited Villareal at the Estadio El Madrigal for Matchday 4 of the La Liga season, and led his team to an 2-0 win by opening the scoring with a 2nd minute right-footed strike. Cristiano's six goals in his first ever four La Liga appearances made him the First Ever Real Madrid player to score in all his initial four La Liga appearances, with Cristiano having the distinction during the first four consecutive La Liga matches of his debut season. Cristiano's remarkable 8 goals in his first five consecutive games with Real Madrid in the La Liga and the Champions League was another Real Madrid record that he had established. Cristiano was on the pitch for 78 minutes during the Matchday 5 La Liga game at home against Tenerife and was instrumental in helping his team score an 3-0 lead, before being substituted for Mahamadou Diarra when the game was ended on the same scoreline to ensure their winning start to the league with a maximum of 15 points. Cristiano finished September 2009 with playing for 70 minutes in Real Madrid's 2nd Champions League Group C game at home against Marseille and was awarded his second consecutive Champions League Man of the Award for his impressive performance, which saw him alone helping his team win the victory of 3-0 that saw them at the top of the group with a total of six points from two games when he started scoring with a left-footed shot, and provided the assistance for the second score in the first second minute, and finally scored by scoring a right-footed 64th minute shot that completed his 32nd career brace before being rested by Higuain. Cristiano was able to score 4 goals and had provided one assist, for a total of five direct goal involvement during his first two appearances in the UEFA Champions League for Real Madrid. Cristiano finished the month of September by scoring 10 goals as well as one assist, for a total of 11 direct goal participations in the duration of 432 minutes over 6 games with Real Madrid, and with 180 minutes of playing for Portugal.

Because of an injury to his ankle suffered during training on the 1st of October 2009

Cristiano did not play in Real Madrid's initial match of the month, three days later, when they lost 2-1 to Sevilla because of lack of the top-of-the-line Most Goal-Scorer and Top Player. Although he felt much better a week after the injury Captain Cristiano did manage to get Portugal started in their 9th 2010. World Cup Qualifier at home against Hungary on the 10th of October 2009, and helped lead players to win a convincing 3-0 victory with his assist on their opener at the end of 27 minutes, before being dismissed at the same time following a second serious ankle injurythat prevented him from playing for a period of more than one month and two weeks. The injury led Cristiano to be out for both games in Portugal's World Cup European Qualification Playoffs against Bosnia-Herzegovina and Bosnia-Herzegovina, which his team were victorious with the score of 2-0 in aggregate to secure their spot for the South Africa 2010 FIFA World Cup. The team, however, Real Madrid missed the Portugal Captain more as even though they won a victory in the league by 4-2 against Real

Valladolid on October 17 the 17th of October, 2009, they lost 3-2 in their home game against AC Milan on October 21 on the Champions League, following that with a disappointing draw of 0-0 against Sporting Gijon on October 24 2009, in league. following which they were beaten 4-0 by Alcorcon at the end of the Copa del Rey first game, before rebounding with a 2-0 win at home against Getafe on October 31st of 2009 in the league. It was then a draw of 1-1 away from AC Milan on November 3 2009 during the Champions League, and then an impressive 3-2 opening Madrid Derby of the season victory over Atletico Madrid in November 7 in the league. Following an unhelpful win of 1-0 at home against Alcorcon during the Copa del Rey game which means that Real Madrid had been eliminated from the tournament with an aggregate of 4-1 for the entire season. Then, finally winning 1-0 at home against Racing Santander in the league on the 21st of November in 2009. Cristiano was back from injury in November 25th, 2009 and only played 20 minutes in the Real

Madrid's home victory over Zurich during their 5th Champions League Group C game that saw them remain at the top of the group by ten points. In November 29th, 2009 Cristiano ended the month by playing just 65 minutes during the game of his Classico debut at Barcelona in the Camp Nou for their Matchday 12 game of the La Liga season, during which he displayed his outstanding ability to play football and earned his the Man of the Match Award during his Classico debut. He was substituted by Benzema at the end of 65 minutes. Real Madrid was beaten 1-0 by Barcelona in a highly tense game where both teams were awarded a yellow card for each. For the months of October and November 2009 Cristiano was on the pitch for 85 minutes during two appearances for Real Madrid, and provided one assist in 27 minutes of his game for Portugal.

Cristiano began the month of December 2009 with no injuries during an at-home La Liga Matchday 13 game against Almeria on December 5, 2009 and was the player who assisted the goal that opened the game in the 31st minutes that earned them a 1-0 opening half victory. However, despite failing to score a penalty in second half and bouncing back, he scored a closing the scoring with an 84th minute right-footed strike that gave his team a win of 2-1. Following his celebration of the goal, he getting his shirt removed after which he was penalized and then the Catalonian referee handed the player another yellow card 3 minutes later and sent the player out. A few days later Cristiano was playing the entire last Champions League Group C game at the Stade Velodrome against Marseille and won the third time in a row for his Champions League Man of the award, after helping his team win victory by scoring a 3-1 win. He opened scoring in the 5th minute with a direct free-kick and then providing the help for their second score during the 60th minute, before closing the scoring in the 80th minute, with a right-footed strike, which allowed the team to move four points ahead of the highest level of the group with 14 points. This performance signified that Cristiano scored six goals, three of which were free kicks that were direct, and he also contributed 2 assists to the total of eight direct goal involvements in the game, which lasted 270 minutes over four Champions League Group Stage appearances as well as winning the Man of the Match Award throughout the games. The goal was Cristiano's 32nd of career. On the 20th of December, 2009 Cristiano ended 2009 with all of Real Madrid's final game of the year. It was the Matchday 15 La Liga game at home against Real Zaragoza, and scoring the fifth goal of the game with a left-footed 50th minute shot. The hosts took the game the game 6-0, bringing their points total for league play at the close of the year at 37. Cristiano completed December 2009 with a record-breaking four goals and two assists, totalling six direct goal involvement in 267 minutes of appearances with Real Madrid in the La Liga as well as in the Champions League. Cristiano thus ended with the distinction of being an Real Madrid player with 13 goals and 4 assists , for total 17 direct goal involvements in 874 minutes over 12 appearances. That means that he scored 1 goals every 67.23 minutes, 1 assistance every 218.5 minutes, and 1 directly involved goal each 51.41 minutes. Cristiano finished the year with club-specific statistics for football of nine assists and 39 goals totaling 50 direct involvement over 3394 minutes of 42 appearances with Manchester United and Real Madrid which is an average of 1 goal per 87.03 minutes, and an involvement of one goal in each 70.71 minutes. In addition to his 1 assist over 387 minutes during five competitive games in the national team of Portugal during the course of 2009, he concluded the year with 39 assists and 9 goals, for total 49 direct goal involvements in 3781 minutes during 47 appearances in competition with Manchester United, Real Madrid and Portugal in an average of one goal per 96.95 minutes and one direct goal participation per 77.16 minutes. Cristiano's goal in two games for Portugal in the course of the year meant the year ended with 10 assists and 40 goals over 3928 minutes of 49 games with Manchester United, Real Madrid and Portugal.

for his outstanding performance as a Wing-Midfielder, who transformed to become a Wing forward the only difference being his defensive role was restricted to corners and free-kicks and a situation that the Ultimate Footballer frequently utilized with his incredible speed and speed in executing devastating counter-attacks in the middle of defense, or midfield. After helping to defend set-pieces. Cristiano was selected for the second occasion as being one of the three best forwards to play in World Football in the 2009 FIFPro World XI and was also named to the 2009 UEFA Team of the Year for the fourth and the third time as one of the four best midfielders on the field in European Football. Cristiano was named the Second-Best player of 2009 when he was named to his way to the Podium at the FIFA World Player of the Year Award and was awarded the Podium as the Second Best in the France Football Ballon D'Or; and won the 2nd Most

Outstanding Of All Time d'Argent Award at the Onze Mondial Awards. Although he had been released from Manchester United, Cristiano's outstanding performance during his time at the club continued receiving him individual awards as he was awarded the 2009. FIFA Puskas Award for the best goal during World Football between July 2008 between July 2008 and July 2009. This was his awe-inspiring sixth minute goal, the 40-yard line in Manchester United's 1-0 victory against Porto during the 2008/09 Champions League Quarterfinals. Cristiano played in the 2009 Sports Illustrated Team of the Decade and was awarded three consecutive CNID Best Portuguese Athlete Abroad Award for 2009. Cristiano's individual awards for the year's end of 2008 along with being awarded the 2008-09 PFA Player of the Year appearance and the 2008/09 Manchester United Goal of the Season Award saw him finish in 2009 having won 10 different accolades. Cristiano's team honours for 2009 included three overall, which included The English Premier League, the EFL Cup and the

Champions League Second Third. In 2009, Cristiano had donated 120,000 pounds to the hospital which had successfully treated his mother's cancer. This meant that the possibility of a cancer center was built on his island Madeira to give local patients with access to top quality health care.

Cristiano started the new year 2010 by playing the entire La Liga Matchday 16 game of the season. It was the 3rd of January, 2010 game at the Estadio El Sader as Real Madrid played against Osasuna who kept them to an 0-0 draw. On the 10th of January 10, 2010, Cristiano was on the field for the entire match during the match as Real Madrid hosted Mallorca for Matchday 17 and led his team score a winning 2-0. On the 17th of January 17, 2010, Cristiano was a full participant during the Matchday 18 La Liga visit to Athletic Bilbao's Estadio San Mames, and despite being the best player in the match, Real Madrid lost 1-0. On the 20th of January 20, 2010, Cristiano took home his fourth friendlies award of the year when Real

Madrid won the Taci Oil Cup by defeating Gramozi Erseke 2-1 at the Qemal Stafa Stadium. On the 24th of January of 2010, Cristiano began his debut as a player for Real Madrid as they hosted Malaga for their La Liga Matchday 19 game and beat the hosts with two goal in the game's 2-0 win with right-footed shots during both the 39th and 35th minutes . This made it the 33rd goal of his career. He was handed a scathing penalty in the 70th minutes after striking an opponent whom he was pulling in the 70th minute after the ball had passed the opponent and was headed for the goal. Cristiano completed January with two goals over four appearances for 340 minutes with Real Madrid. But, Cristiano ended the month with relief when his lawyers finally got the signing of a Non-Disclosure agreement worth $375,000 from an American woman who took advantage of the one-night-stand opportunity together to their maximum advantage to get the money , with the condition that she not go everywhere with her false accusations which could have harmed Cristiano's image, reputation and professional career. But, he'd learned his lesson, and it is one that all professional and aspiring athletes as well as celebrities can all take a note from.

Cristiano began his second month in the new Year by turning 25 on the 5th of February 2010. After eight days, Cristiano returned to action as Real Madrid visited Xerex for La Liga's Matchday 22, and played all game long while celebrating his birthday on the field as he made the first goal of the game with a header in 69th minute . He then scored by scoring their third goal with an unintentionally left-footed shot in the 71st minute that gave his team the victory 3-0, and the brace was his 34th goal of his career. The two-time La Liga strike was his second goal in two consecutive La Liga matches. On February 16 2010 Cristiano was a full participant in the match as Real Madrid travelled to the Stade de Gerland for the first Leg in their Champions League Round of 16 match against Lyon losing 1-1. On February 24 the 24th of February, 2010 Cristiano was the sole player in the Real Madrid's La Liga Matchday 23 game on the pitch against Villareal and led the team in a 6-1 success with his first goal at the end of 17 minutes with an unintentional free-kick. He then followed that with showing his excellent playmaking skills with a hat-trick assist for the third goal, fifth and sixth during the 54th, 79th, and the 87th minute. on February 27th, 2010 Cristiano ended the month by taking part in every minute of the Real Madrid's Matchday 24 visit to the Estadio Hellodoro Rodriguez Lopez against Tenerife and was able to put up excellent performance. He also scored the seventh consecutive goal in direct involvement. He scored an impressive fourth strike of February. Cristiano scored Real Madrid's 4th goal in the game with a penalty in the 80th minute with a final score of 5-1. Cristiano completed the month with four goals and three assists over 360 minutes of games with Real Madrid in the La Liga as well as in the Champions League.

Cristiano started March 2010 as Captain Cristiano by kicking off and encouraging Portugal in a 2-0 victory against China in an March 3 2010 international friendly held at the Estadio Dr. Magalhaes Pessoa in Portugal. He assisted on their opener at the end of 36 minutes, before being rested at the conclusion of the first period for Liedson. On March 6 in 2010, Cristiano was on the pitch for the entire game in the match as Real Madrid hosted Sevilla for La Liga's Matchday 25 and helped his team win an 3-2 win.

coming back victory that secured the team top position with a comeback victory that secured them top spot in La Liga with 62 points at the time of scoring. He opened the scoring for the hosts with a left-footed shot in the 59th minute which was his seventh consecutive goal in his five La Liga appearances to half the lead of 2-0 for the visitors prior to helping his team get an equalizer in the 66th minute and a 90th+2 minutes match-winner. On the 10th of March 2010 in a full match performance, Cristiano tried inspiring Real Madrid to win against Lyon in the second Leg in their Champions League Round of 16 match at home. He scored the opener in the 6th minute, however the goal was not equalized until the 75th minute, and the match ended in a draw that led to the Real Madrid's exile of their participation in the Champions League by a 2-1 loss on aggregate. Cristiano scored the seventh Champions League goal of the season. This, along with the 2 assists he contributed, the 2010/10 Champions League season with 9 direct goal-related involvements in the 450 minutes he played in six games that made him the most efficient player during this Champions League season, as the average was one goal per 64.29 minutes, and one direct goal participation every 50 minutes during all of the Champions League season. Seven goals in just six appearances was impressive enough to make him the 2nd Top Goal-Scorer in the Champions League season with just one goal less than the total of the final most prolific scorer in the tournament, Messi, who played another six games. On March 14 in 2010, Cristiano was a full participant in the match as Real Madrid visited the Estadio Jose Zorilla to play Real Valladolid in their La Liga match on Matchday 26, and he helped his team win the victory of 4-1 by scoring via a direct shot in the 29th minute, and after that, he assisted on real Madrid's fourth and third goals. Thanks to his efforts Cristiano was able to help Real Madrid to their eighth consecutive La Liga win, which kept them in the top spot having earned 65 points. Cristiano's goal means he has scored eight goals in six consecutive La Liga appearances that in addition to his five assists. This meant that he had 13 consecutive direct goals in six consecutive La Liga appearances. In addition to the Champions League goal, Cristiano scored five goals in a row as well as providing 5 assists, for 10 straight direct goal involvement in five consecutive appearances with Real Madrid in La Liga and the Champions League.

On the 20th of March 2010 Cristiano was on the pitch for the entire game while bringing his playmaking abilities to the forefront as he contributed assists to his team's equalizing goal , and the second goal in their 3-1 win at home against Sporting Gijon in their La Liga Matchday 27 game. His spirited performance resulted in real madrid's 9th consecutive league victory and helped them remain in the the top spot, with the score of 68 points. Two assists meant that the player had contributed a pair of assists in two consecutive La Liga matches, and added 15 consecutive direct goals in seven consecutive La Liga appearances and 12 direct goals in six consecutive games with Real Madrid. On March 25 the 25th of March, 2010 Cristiano took part in the entire game in the match as Real Madrid visited the Coliseum Alfonso Perez to lock horns with Getafe on Matchday 28 and led his team to the victory of 4-2, which was their tenth consecutive win in league and boosted their point total to top spot on the league table, with 71 points. The team opened scoring via a direct goal from the free-kick at 13 minutes after that, closing the scoring by scoring a right-footed 36th minute shot that clinched the 35th brace of his career. This performance signified that he scored 10 goals in a row and had contributed seven assists, thereby getting 17 straight direct goals in eight consecutive La Liga appearances. Also, the goals signified that he'd scored 14 consecutive direct goals during 7 consecutive games in the Champions League and La Liga. Real Madrid in La Liga as well as the Champions League. On March 28 in 2010, Cristiano completed the month by making the debut of his Madrid Derby debut in their La Liga Matchday 29 game in which he played every minute of the game while they defeated their city opponents, Atletico Madrid, by the score of 3-2. This was their 11th consecutive league win , which added points to 74, which is the highest point in the table. Cristiano thus ended the month of March 2010 with five goals and 4 assists in five appearances in the Champions League and La Liga for Real Madrid in La Liga as well as The Champions League, and with one assist in a 45-minute game for Portugal.

Cristiano started the month of April with his full-time appearance at the Real Madrid's La Liga Matchday 30 game at the Campos of Sport de Sardinero against Racing Santander on April 4 in 2010. He was a key player who helped his team to win their 12-game streak of La Liga win, as Cristiano opened the game by assisting after being fouled and converted the penalty at the end of the 23rd minutes to help them win 2-0 away that saw Real Madrid top of the league with 77 points. On April 10 10, 2010, Cristiano was in the full match of the Matchday 31 fixture as Real Madrid's title hopes suffered by a devastating home defeat of 2-0 against Barcelona during the 2nd Classico in the league which saw them fall to second within the competition. This was the final match of the two biggest competitions in Spanish football, which involved Cristiano during the 2009/10 season as the player ended his appearances with them by winning the Classico Man of the Match award. On

April 15, 2010, Cristiano bounced back with his team by participating in the full game as Real Madrid visited Almeria at the Estadio de Los Juegos Miditerraneos for Matchday 32 and he was a major factor in his team's victory. With his team down 1-0 the score was leveled with a left-footed shot in the 26th minute that led his team to win 2-1 which increased their league point total by 80 to. On April 18 the 18th of April, 2010 Cristiano was a full participant in the match as Real Madrid hosted Valencia in their La Liga Matchday 33 game and was a key part of the team's victory by scoring the winner with a right-footed strike that added points to their league total to 83. On April 24 the 24th of April, 2010 Cristiano completed the month with a full game as Real Madrid visited Zaragoza at the La Romareda Stadium for their La Liga Matchday 34 encounter and, in a demonstration of his ability to play provided assists for the team's two goals when they beat Zaragoza 2-1 to keep their second place in the league, with the score of 86 points. Cristiano completed April 2010 with three goals and three assists in 450 minutes of five La Liga appearances for Real Madrid.

Cristiano started the month of May by playing all match and guiding Real Madrid to a 3-2 home win against Osasuna the 2nd of May in the La Liga Matchday 35 game in the league season. when his team was down 1-1, he scored an equalizer in the 25th minute with a right-footed shot. With the score tied at 2-2 He sealed the match with an 90th minute header that sealed an impressive 36-year career with a brace. This allowed his team to win their fourth straight La Liga win that increased the total of their league points to 89. On May 5 2010 Cristiano was the first player to start his Real Madrid's Matchday 36 La Liga game at the Iberostar Estadi against Mallorca and, after the hosts had scored after the first half, he scored his second league game in succession with an right-footed shot in the 26th minute and then scored the following two goals of the game with right-footed strikes in the 56th and 71st minute for Real Madrid a commanding 3-1 lead. After aiding the team to the lead of 4-1 and a 4-1 lead, he was substituted to Benzema during the final minute of the match of the match. The game ended with the same scoreline , which helped raise their points total for the league to 92, which is second in the league. The three goals that were right-footed meant Cristiano was able to score his first hat-trick in Real Madrid and in his La Liga career. This was the second hat-trick in his career, and it meant he had scored a hat-trick with the teams of Manchester United and Real Madrid and also in the English Premier League and the Spanish La Liga. On May 8, 2010, Cristiano played the full match when Real Madrid hosted Athletic Bilbao in their La Liga Matchday 37 game of the season. He helped his team win 5-1 victory after scoring in the 22nd-minute penalty that brought the total of their league points to 95. On May 16, 2010, Cristiano played the entirety of Real Madrid's last match of the La Liga season against relegation-threatened Malaga at the Estadio La Rosaleda, which had little meaning after Barcelona had already won the La Liga title earlier in the day, and helped his team to a 1-1 draw, a much-needed result for a determined Malaga team that helped them secure La Liga football for the next season. The draw meant that Real Madrid had ended the La Liga season in second spot with 96 points. This was only 3 points off the Champions, and was automatically advancing to the Group Stage of the 2010/11 UEFA Champions League. Cristiano finished the month of May with six goals in 353 minutes of his four La Liga appearances.

In this 2009/10 La Liga season, Cristiano was the Real Madrid's most direct Goal Involvements Acquirer with 37 direct goals and their top assister with 11 assists, and Second-highest Goal Scorer with 26 goals, only one goal less than Higuain in the span of 2461 minutes over 29 games at an average of 1 goals every 94.65 minutes, 1-assist every 223.73 minutes, and one direct goal-related involvement each 65.51 minute. Cristiano alone was involved in 36.27 percent from the Real Madrid's La Liga season best 102 goals.

At the top of the La Liga, Cristiano was the second Direct Goal Involvements Acquirer with 37 direct goal involvements just behind Messi at 43. The Second-Highest Assists Provider, with 11 assists, compared to Xavi with 13 assists. He was also the third top goal scorer who scored 26 times, following Messi who scored 34 goals and Higuain at 27. Cristiano's performance throughout his first year with La Liga was very impressive since he was the most Effective player in the league, scoring one goal every 94.65 minutes, and one direct goal involvement each 65.51 minute. In the entire 2009/10 season Cristiano was the top Real Madrid Goalscorer with 33 goals, Top Assists Provider, with 13 assists; and the most Direct Goal Involvements Acquirer with 46 direct goals which meant he was direct involved with 38.98 percent of the 118 goals scored by Real Madrid during 2911 minutes of 35 Real Madrid appearances for the whole season , in all competitions. This means that he scored 1 goal per 88.21 minutes, 1 assistance every 223.92 minutes, and 1 Direct Goal

Involvement in every 63.28 minutes, both in both the Champions League and La Liga. Cristiano's statistics for 2009/10 of one goals per 88.21 minutes and a direct goal-related involvement every 63.28 minutes earned him the title of most effective footballer for the entire season in European Football throughout the season.

7.5. CAPTAIN CRISTIANO RONALDO CONCLUDS the 2011/12 SEASON as the most effective and most EFFECTIVE Player in World Football INSPIRING PORTUGAL TO WIN BRONZE at EURO 2012 AS HE EARNS 2 MAN of the Match AWARDS and A PLACE in the TEAM OF THE TOURNAMENT

While Cristiano's football season had been over the 2011/12 season wasn't finished as he was required to be the captain of his team for the 2012 European Championship that was jointly hosted by Ukraine and Poland. To prepare for the event that took place in the Netherlands, Portugal was assigned to the "Group of Death" together with Germany and

The Netherlands as well as Turkey, Cristiano played 73 minutes before being substituted by Silvestre Varela during Portugal's second consecutive draw without goals during an international friendly against Macedonia in the Estadio Dr. Magalhaes Pessoa on the 26th of May 2012. Two days later, on June 2nd 2012 Cristiano was part of the entire international match on the Estadio da Luz against Turkey losing 3-1 that included a missed a penalty but was able to make the right decision, and in the team falling 2-0. He was the one to assist their sole goal at the end of the game in the 56th minute. The appearance at the international level was the final appearance of Cristiano for the year in which he concluded the 2011/12 season with a goal and 2 assists over 284 minutes during 4 international games. In June 9th, 2012 Captain Cristiano was the captain of Portugal throughout the entire 90 minutes during their initial EURO 2012 Group B game at the Arena Lviv, Ukraine against Germany that ended in an 1-0 loss for Portugal. The 13th of June 2012 Captain Cristiano took part in the entire the two-game EURO 2012 game at the Arena Lviv, and led Portugal to their first EURO 2012 win over Denmark when the game ended 3-2. On the 17th of June 2012 Captain Cristiano received his First Man of the Match Award at EURO 2012 in their final Group B game with the Netherlands on the OSK Metalist Stadium in Kharkiv, Ukraine, as when Portugal being down by 1-0, he, his role as the Ultimate Big Game Player, scored the equalizing goal through an unorthodox shot in the 28th minute and then completed his 56th career goal by finishing the game with his right-footed goal in the 74th minute following a dribble from his opponent's right-back down to the ground. The match-winning brace was his seventh of his international career which gave his team the win 2-1 and a place to the Quarterfinals at EURO 2012.

The 21st of June, 2012 Captain Cristiano was on the field for each minute in Portugal's quarterfinal Game against Czech Republic at the PGE Marodowy Stadium in Poland and was awarded the second time in a row EURO

2012 Man of the Match Award. This came in the form of the third EURO Man of the Match award of his international career. He scored a second consecutive match-winner for Portugal with a 79th-minute goal to make Portugal for EURO 2012 Semifinals. In the semi-finals of EURO 2012, Cristiano played every minute of the game as Portugal played against the eventual Champions, Spain, on June 27 in 2012 at the Donbass Arena in Donetsk, Ukraine and inspired his team to put on an energetic performance against a better team who won the previous season of EURO 2008 as well as at the time of the 2010 World Cup to force the match to finish goalless after 90 minutes, and then extra time, which meant that the winner was decided by penalty shootout. The shootout was a penalty shootout Cristiano was supposed to get the fifth penalty, but his teammates missed two penalties and were defeated 4-2 before he had the chance to claim his. In the semi-finals, UEFA awarded Bronze Medals to the Semifinalists who were defeated as a result. Cristiano received the third highest international soccer distinction following winning his EURO 2004 Silver Medal and Fourth Place Place during the 2006 World Cup. Cristiano finished EURO 2012 with 3 goals in 480 minutes over five matches, and concluded EURO 2012 with the same goals scored in Cristiano was the EURO 2012 Golden Boot Award winner. Cristiano was the winner of the EURO 2012 Top Goal Scorer Distinction. He also won two Men of the Match Awards and an appearance in the EURO 2012 Team of the Tournament being selected two times in his life. He did this after being a part of in the EURO 2004 tournament.

It was the EURO 2012 Bronze Medal was Cristiano's fourth team international distinction since turning professional following his Toulon tournament Gold Medal EURO 2004 Silver Medal and the 2006 World Cup Fourth Place Finish. In addition, the two EURO 2012 Man of the Match Awards and his participation as a member of the EURO 2012 Team of the Tournament added his international football individual honours to 8 after he was a part of EURO 2004's EURO 2004 Team of the Tournament and earned one EURO 2008 Man of the Match Award and 3 2010 World Cup Man of the Match Awards. The EURO 2012 performances meant that Cristiano scored six goals and had provided five assists in 1180 minutes of fourteen EURO performances in his career, scoring in all three editions, and earning five individual awards. Alongside his general FIFA World Cup career statistics of two goals and an assist in 844 minutes over 10 appearances, after taking part and scoring in two consecutive editions of the world championship, Cristiano had therefore scored 8 goals and had provided 6 assists over 2024 minutes over 24 appearances in The European Championship and the FIFA World Cup as a Big Game player and a Major Tournament Player, he had scored in each of five successive seasons of the most prestigious senior international football tournaments, since the time of his with the senior international team. In his international appearances in competition for the 2011/12 season Cristiano had scored eight goals and given 1 assist over ninety minutes of playing time in 10 appearances. This, added to the statistics of his season with Real Madrid meant that he finished his 2011/12 season as the world's best and Most Effective player with scores of 72 goals and 17 assists and direct goal involvement of 89 during 6008 minutes across 68 appearances in the competitive season. That means he concluded the season in a competitive fashion with the average of 1 goals every 83.44 minutes, and a direct goal each 67.51 minutes during the Champions League, the World Football Challenge, La Liga as well as the Copa del Rey, the Spanish Super Cup, the EURO 2012 Qualifiers and EURO 2012. Cristiano's one goal and two assists over 284 minutes during four international friendlies which meant he finished the entire 2011/12 season for both country and club with 19 assists and 73 goals over 6292 minutes of matches with Real Madrid and Portugal.

Cristiano's outstanding performance during the season, which made him both the Top

Player and the Most Effective Player at the top of World Football and had inspired his team as well as National to be awarded team honours and resulted in the second time in his career Goal 50 Award; his first ever Alfredo di Stefano Trophy; an EURO 2012 Team of the Tournament appearance and Two EURO 2008 Man of the Match Awards as well as an EURO 2012 Top Goal Scorer Distinction and the ESM team of the Season appearance; an UEFA Most Valuable Player Europe joint Second-Place Podium appearance, along with Messi and Messi; and the second-place Podium participation during the Onze Mondial Awards as winner of the Onze d'Argent Award along with the seven individual awards, he finished the year with sixteen individual awards. After three years of leaving the Premier League, Cristiano's great performances in his six seasons as an Manchester United Player there earned him recognition during the English Premier League 20 Seasons Awards in which he was included as a member of the Premier League Public Choice Fantasy Team of the 20 Seasons and also the Panel Choice Team of the 20 Seasons. Cristiano was also among the 10 nominees for the Best player of 20 Seasons Award. In addition his 2007/08 Manchester Team, of which Cristiano was the best Goal-Scorer and the Top Direct Goal Involvements Acchiever of the team was selected as one of the five teams to be the winner of the Top team in the 20 Seasons Award. Cristiano's two English Premier League 20 Seasons Awards awards increased his personal honours to 17. The 2011/12 campaign of Cristiano was an impressive one as he did well at the highest level of Club Football as well as International Football, inspiring Real Madrid to win the Spanish La Liga title and victory in the World Football Challenge, and as well as inspiring and leading Portugal towards Bronze during EURO 2012, to end the season with three team awards.

7.8. CAPTAIN Cristiano RONALDO SUCCESSFULLY FINISHES his 2013/14 SEASON WITH an HONORABLE performance for an UNFORTUNATE Portugal's participation in the 2014. FIFA WORLD CUP DESPITE BEING injured as he scores in a SIXTH SUCCESSIVE SENIOR INTERNATIONAL TOURNAMENT and earns one more WORLD CUP Man of the Match Award

The club season was over in spite of Cristiano suffering from patellar tendinitis as well as an associated thigh injury the possibility arose that he could risk his career by choosing to disregard medical advice, and join the Portuguese team to participate in 2014's FIFA World Cup hosted by Brazil. In response to questions about why he chosen to put at risk his career once again within a month, having previously participated in in the UEFA Champions League through a similar injury, he answered by saying "If there were three or four Cristiano Ronaldos on the squad (Portugal national team) I'd feel more secure. However, we don't". So, as Portugal's Top player and the best player at European as well as World Football, who would be extremely missed by his team who usually faced tough times without him. He was not able to let his team and fellow countrymen down at a time when they needed him the most, even though he could risk his career by taking a risk to his team and country during the match. Because of the poor condition of his injury, he had to stop practice twice, due to persistent doubts over his fitness for his third FIFA World Cup participation. In June 2011, trying to heal the injury as best the medical team and he could and did, Captain Cristiano took part in 65 minutes of Portugal's final World Cup preparatory game against the Republic of Ireland on June 11 at the MetLife Stadium in East Rutherford, New Jersey, and played the team score an early 3-0 lead. He was substituted by Nani after the game ended with a 5-0 win, that showed the effect his presence played on the team every time was on the field in the past. Portugal were unable to win in their previous two World Cup warm-up matches without their legendary Captain. On June 16 14th, 2014, despite his injury Captain Cristiano was able to play the entire 90 minutes of Portugal's opening group G game in the 2014 FIFA World Cup against Germany at the Arena Fonte Nova, which was marked by a red card to his co-player and fellow Real Madrid teammate and the most outstanding Portuguese defensive player, Pepe, for unnecessary aggressive behavior that led to an injury that Germany scored to move ahead 1-0 before three more goals scored by Germany because of the extremely weak Portuguese defense, which led to an 4-0 victory for Germany.

On the 23rd of June on the 23rd of June in 2014 Captain Cristiano was on the field for each minute in Portugal's first Group G match in the 2014 World Cup at the Arena da Amazonia against the United States of America in spite of a stern warning by the medical staff, when his team was in a 2-1 deficit, he demonstrated that he was a valuable player to his team while playing with injury providing his team with their first goal of the tournament by providing the assistance for the equalizer goal in the 90th minute after the match ended in a draw which helped keep their hopes of qualifying to the Knockout Phase of the tournament alive. On June 26th the 26th of June, 2014 Captain Cristiano was the sole player in Portugal's 3rd Brazil 2014 World Cup Group G game at the Estadio Nacional Mane Garrincha de Brasilia against Ghana with the score being 1-1, he offered reasons the reason he is regarded as the greatest footballer of all time as well as a natural and great leader, and the best ever Portuguese Soccer player by scoring Portugal's game-winning goal with an 80th-minute left-footed strike to ensure the team ultimately took the win by 2-1. It was Cristiano's 50th goal in his career as an international footballer and also made him the first Ever Portuguese to play and score three FIFA World Cup editions. The goal also brought Cristiano four FIFA World Man of the Match Award. But even with the captain Cristiano having made a huge sacrifice to his country in the role of a great Patriot by playing through injuries and allowing his team to earn all the points they earned at the 2014 World Cup, Portugal unfortunately was not able to make it to the Knockout stage of the tournament by goals scored. Cristiano's goal and assist in his two consecutive 2014 World Cup appearances meant he finished the 2014 FIFA World Cup participation with one goal and one assist over 270 minutes in three appearances. Cristiano scored his 50th goal in his career for internationals and made him the first and only Portuguese Goalscorer to score in three World Cups.

The match resulted in Cristiano's overall FIFA World Cup statistics stood at 3 goals and 2 assists in 1114 minutes over the 13 World Cup appearances in 3 consecutive years. In addition, the Man of the Match Award was his fourth Man of the Match Award at the FIFA World Cup in only the second year of the tournament when the awards made offered. Cristiano has scored goals during all six consecutive seasons of the senior international football tournaments starting from EURO 2004 to the 2014 FIFA World Cup to put his international tournaments of senior level stats as 9 assists, 7 goals along with seven man of the Match Awards within nine individual awards over 2294 minutes of 27 appearances at three successive European Championships and 3 consecutive FIFA World Cups. Cristiano's stats for competitive play include 8 goals as well as one assist in 630 minutes of seven appearances for Portugal during the entire season along with his stats for competitive play with Real Madrid meant that he finished the 2013/14 season with 19 assists and 62 goals with a total of 81 direct goal participations in 4864 minutes of his 57 appearances. This means that there was an average of 1.25 goals every 78.45 minutes and one direct goal participation each 60.05 minutes. Alongside the 3 goals and 1 assist over 245 minutes in two international friendly matches in the national team of Portugal, Cristiano ended the 2013/14 season with a record of 65 goal and 20 assist over 5109 minutes of appearances in 59 games for Real Madrid and Portugal. He was awarded the 2014 World Cup Man of the Match Award signified that Cristiano finished the 2013/14 season with 25 individual accolades. Cristiano finished the season with his Champions League, the Copa del Rey and the

International Champions Cup as team honours. On June 14, 2014 Cristiano uploaded a video on Vimeo called Cristiano Ronaldo A World of His Feet that was read by Hollywood actor, Benedict Cumberbatch.

7.13. CAPTAIN CRISTIANO ROLANDO CONCLUDING HIS 2016/17 season by welcoming HIS twins and leading Portugal to the BRONZE MEDAL IN HIS first ever participation the FIFA CONFEDERATIONS CUP , WHILE WINNING 3 MAN of the Match AWARDS

After Cristiano's season at the club was over however, his time at the club was not finished because he was required to take charge of the National Team in a 2018 World Cup European Qualifiers game as well as lead the team at the 2017 Confederations Cup that was hosted by Russia. Portugal was able to participate in the tournament in the role of UEFA National Team Champions after winning the 2016 European Championship the previous summer and was required to go up against

179

counterparts in the form of Champion competitors from FIFA's other confederations as well as being the World Champions and the host nation. On June 8 on the same day, five days after bringing Real Madrid to Champions League glory by scoring a brace in the final Cristiano has become the dad of two more twins, twins Eva Maria and son Mateo Ronaldo and Mateo Ronaldo, both of whom were born via surrogacy in the United States of America. Cristiano was not able to be present with his new babies because on the next day, on June 9th the 9th of June, 2017, he was forced to take on the role of captain Cristiano and played all of the time in Portugal's 5th World Cup. World Cup European Qualifier against Latvia at the Skonto Stadium in Riga. He maintained his excellent form for Portugal's National Team, as he began scoring by scoring a header in the 41st minute followed by doubling the lead in the 63rd minute with a header to score his 103rd career brace and then assisting on the goal that ended the game at the end of the game in the 67th minutes to give his team a win of 3-0 with three goals directly involved. The brace signified it was the first time Cristiano has scored goals in all six of Portugal's games he participated in during the season with 12 goals scored during this year's FIFA Confederations Cup.

On the 18th of June in 2017 Captain Cristiano was on the field for every minute of the game when he commanded Portugal to victory in the First Ever FIFA Confederations Cup match in Kazan Arena. Kazan Arena against Mexico, and attempted to lead the team to victory by helping to score the first goal of the game after having defeated Mexico's entire Mexican defense. He then passed on the ball for Quaresma to score an unmarked goal however the match ended in the draw of 2-2. Cristiano's exceptional performance during the match brought him an award of the "Man of Match Award in his FIFA Confederations Cup debut, that means he has earned the award for the Man of the Match Award in every major international senior football tournament ever since EURO 2008. On the 21st of June 21, 2017 Captain Cristiano was the sole player in the second FIFA Confederations Cup match against Russia at the Otkrytiye Arena in Moscow, and was the sole person to secure his team victory, scoring the only goal of the game with an eight minute goal in the game as they beat Russia 1-1. Cristiano's outstanding performance in the match brought him a second consecutive man of the Match Award in the tournament.

Conclusion

Here you go. Statistics, facts, and the stories of perhaps the most famous footballer of all time.

It's quite remarkable to look at all the awards and accomplishments and to think that one person could have accomplished the amount. It's impossible to make up even if you tried. It's even more amazing considering that he's still young at just 31. The records are likely to be broken more. In the past, injury-free, he may continue for up to six or five years. And what happens next? What records could be broken? Who knows.

As getting older, his temper has become more even. He's an all-round better player and if he shed the arrogance and anger (which He claims is not arrogance, but rather an aggressive nature) He could be able to improve even more.

And, if it was, would this really be Cristiano Ronaldo? It wouldn't. It's a repeat of Messi. It's not a problem having a second Messi. He's a great footballer; one of the best players in the world. We all are aware of that. However, he would not be Cristiano Ronaldo is not he? And we'll require Cristiano Ronaldos all over the world. No. Scratch that. We only need THE Cristiano Ronaldo of the world.

Printed in the USA
CPSIA information can be obtained
at www.ICGtesting.com
LVHW022030220923
758905LV00013B/979